PRESERVE the HARVEST

Tips and Techniques for Vegetables

Becky M. Wade

Table of Contents

Introduction

Benefits of Vegetable Preservation

Saving vegetables offers a few advantages, including:

Broadened time frame of realistic usability: Conservation strategies like canning, freezing, and drying assist vegetables with enduring longer, decreasing food squandering.

Supplement Maintenance: Appropriate safeguarding strategies can assist with holding fundamental supplements in vegetables, guaranteeing they stay nutritious.

Cost Reserve funds: Purchasing and protecting vegetables in mass can be practical, particularly when they are in-season and more affordable.

Comfort: Saved vegetables are promptly accessible for use in cooking, making feast arrangements more advantageous.

Occasional Pleasure: You can partake in your number one vegetable all year, in any event, when they're unavailable.

Crisis Readiness: Saved vegetables can be a significant piece of crisis food supplies.

Manageability: Decreasing food waste and dependence on unavailable produce can be all the more earth-reasonable.

Flavor and Taste: A few safeguarded vegetables, similar to pickles and matured items, foster novel flavors over the long haul.

Assortment: Protection permits you to try different things with a large number of vegetable assortments, including treasure and uncommon choices that may not be promptly accessible.

Customization: You have some control over the fixings and flavorings utilized during conservation, fitting the taste as you would prefer.

Decrease in Synthetic Substances: Hand-crafted conservation strategies frequently include fewer added substances and synthetic compounds contrasted with financially handled food sources.

Decrease of Food Decay: Conservation lessens the possibility of vegetables ruining before you can utilize them, guaranteeing you benefit from your staple buys.

Reasonable Agribusiness: Supporting neighborhood and occasional vegetable safeguarding energizes feasible cultivating rehearses.

Pre-arranged Fixings: Saved vegetables can act as pre-arranged elements for speedy and simple cooking.

Culinary Imagination: Protecting vegetables can motivate inventiveness in the kitchen as you investigate various recipes and utilizations for safeguarded produce.

Medical advantages: Eating vegetables consistently, including protected ones, is related to various medical advantages, like diminished hazard of persistent infections.

Learning Open Doors: Vegetable protection can be an instructive and compensating leisure activity, showing you sanitation, science, and conventional culinary methods.

Local area Sharing: You can impart your saved vegetables to loved ones, cultivating a feeling of local area and harmony.

Generally, vegetable safeguarding offers a huge number of benefits that envelop supportability, well-being, and culinary investigation.

Safety Guidelines for Canning

While canning food at home, it's fundamental to keep wellbeing rules to forestall foodborne diseases. Here are some key wellbeing ways to can:

Utilize tried recipes: Just use recipes from dependable sources like the USDA, Public Place for Home Food Protection, or legitimate canning books. Follow them near guarantee legitimate handling times and fixing proportions.

Disinfect gear: Guarantee that containers, tops, and utensils are completely cleaned and disinfected before use.

Utilize fitting canning strategies: There are two principal canning techniques: water shower canning (for high-corrosive food sources like products of the soil) and strain canning (for low-corrosive food varieties like vegetables and meats). Utilize the right strategy for your recipe.

Look at container quality: Examine containers for breaks, chips, or imperfections in the fixing edges. Dispose of any compromised containers.

Select new, top-notch produce: Utilize new, ready produce for canning. Overripe or underripe foods grown from the ground can influence the nature of the result.

Keep up with the right headspace: Leave the suggested space between the food and the highest point of the container to consider appropriate fixing and extension during handling.

Appropriately adapt to elevation: Handling times and tensions might fluctuate with height. Make certain to likewise change your canning technique.

Bubble covers before use: Adhere to the maker's directions to plan covers by stewing them, guaranteeing a decent seal.

Follow handling times and temperatures: Stick to the suggested handling times and temperatures for your particular recipe. Over or under-handling can prompt decay or risky food.

Cool containers appropriately: After handling, permit containers to cool normally on a spotless towel or cooling rack. Try not to move or fix the covers until the containers have completely cooled.

Test seals: Check for fixed tops by pushing down in the middle. If it doesn't pop back, it's appropriately fixed. Any unlocked containers ought to be refrigerated and consumed speedily.

Mark and date your containers: Monitor what's in each container and when it was canned to guarantee you utilize the most established items first.

Store in a cool, dim spot: Once canned, store your containers in a cool, dim, and dry area. Keep away from outrageous temperatures and direct daylight.

By keeping these rules, you can securely appreciate home-canned products for a lengthy period while limiting the gamble of foodborne ailments.

Equipment and Supplies

Canning is an incredible method for safeguarding food. Here are some fundamental hardware and supplies you'll require:

Canning Containers: Artisan bumps or canning containers come in different sizes and are fundamental for putting away the safeguarded food. Covers and Groups: These are utilized to seal the containers. Covers ought to be new and groups can be reused if in great shape.
Canning Pot: An enormous, profound pot with a rack to hold the containers during handling.
Canning Channel: Helps fill containers without spilling.
Top Lifter: To deal with hot covers securely.
Container Lifter: For securely eliminating hot containers from the canner.

Bubble Remover/Debubbler: Used to eliminate air rises from the filled containers.

Estimating devices: To guarantee exact amounts of fixings.

Heat Proof Gloves: Safeguard your hands while taking care of hot containers.

Kitchen Towels: For cleaning and taking care of hot things.

Naming materials: Names, markers, or labels for noticing the items and date of canning.

Corrosive (for certain recipes): Contingent upon what you're canning, you could require citrus extract or lemon juice to keep up with acidity.

Pressure Canner (for low-corrosive food sources): On the off chance that you're canning low-corrosive food varieties like vegetables or meats, a strain canner is important.

Thermometer: To screen the temperature during handling.

Recipe and directions: Follow a trusted canning recipe and rules to guarantee security.

Gelatin (for jams and jams): Assuming you're making jams or jams, you'll require gelatin to assist the blend with setting appropriately.

Sifter or Cheesecloth: Helpful for stressing fluids or eliminating seeds while making natural product jam.

Canning Utensils: Specific utensils with elastic grasps for safely holding hot containers.

Canning Rack or Plate: An instrument to keep containers off the lower part of the canner to forestall breakage.

Container Wrench: Fixes the groups on canning containers.

Wide-Mouth Pipe: Especially helpful for filling wide-mouth containers with thick food sources.

Canning Clock: A kitchen clock can assist you with monitoring handling times precisely.

Margarine Muslin: A fine fabric utilized for stressing, particularly while making cheddar or jam.

Container Brush: Clean the canning containers completely before filling them.

Kitchen Scale: Valuable for estimating exact amounts of elements for recipes.

Make a point to follow legitimate canning strategies and well-being rules to stay away from decay or defilement.

Chapter 1: Understanding Food Preservation Methods

Vegetable Selection and Preparation

Protecting vegetables includes different strategies like canning, freezing, or drying out. Here are a few general strides for determination and planning:

Determination:

Pick new, ready vegetables without imperfections.

Settle on assortments reasonable for protection, such as canning tomatoes or freezing peas.

Washing:

Flush vegetables completely under chilly water to eliminate soil and foreign substances.

Cutting and stripping:

Trim and strip depending on the situation, eliminating any harmed parts.

Cut into proper sizes for your picked protection strategy.

Whitening (for freezing):

Bubble or steam vegetables momentarily, then, at that point, immediately cool in ice water to safeguard tone and surface.

Bundling:

Utilize impermeable holders or vacuum-fixed packs for freezing.

Clean canning containers and tops for canning.

Preparing (discretionary):

Add salt, sugar, or flavors as indicated by your recipe for some zing.

Capacity:

Mark holders with the date and items.

Store in a cool, dim spot for canned products or a cooler for frozen things.

Getting dried out (discretionary):

Utilize a dehydrator or broiler at a low temperature to eliminate dampness for dried vegetables.

Quality check:

Review the vegetables for any indications of decay or sickness before saving them to guarantee the best quality finished result.

Fermentation (for canning):

For low-corrosive vegetables like green beans, add lemon juice or vinegar to safeguard securely and forestall botulism.

Whitening time:u

Follow suggested whitening times for various vegetables; over-whitening can prompt a deficiency of flavor and supplements.

Freezing in segments:

Partition vegetables into segment-measured bundles before freezing, making it simpler to utilize what you want without defrosting the whole clump.

Utilize appropriate gear:

Put resources into quality safeguarding gear, for example, canning packs, vacuum sealers, or a food dehydrator, for improved results and well-being.

Recollect that protected conservation rehearses are fundamental to forestall decay and guarantee the life span of your vegetables. Keep respectable assets and rules intended for your picked safeguarding technique.

Choosing the Best Vegetables

While picking vegetables for safeguarding, consider choices that are new, top-notch, and in season. Ideal decisions frequently include:

Tomatoes: Extraordinary for canning, making sauces, or drying.

Cucumbers: Appropriate for pickling.

Chime peppers: Great for freezing or canning.

Green beans: Great for canning or freezing.

Carrots: Appropriate for canning, pickling, or freezing.

Zucchini: Incredible for pickling, freezing, or making savors.

Corn: Ideal for freezing.

Peas: Reasonable for freezing.

Broccoli and cauliflower: Great for whitening and freezing.

Salad greens like spinach and kale are ideal for whitening and freezing.

Guarantee appropriate handling and stockpiling strategies given the conservation method you pick, whether it's canning, freezing, pickling, or drying.

Beets: Ideal for pickling or canning to make beetroot.

Onions: Reasonable for pickling or making onion savors.

Potatoes: Great for putting away in a cool, dull spot.

Winter squash: Can be put away for a long time in a cool, dry climate.

Asparagus: Great for whitening and freezing.

Radishes: Extraordinary for pickling to make radish pickles.

Eggplant: Appropriate for pickling, making spreads, or freezing.

Green peas: Ideal for canning or making pea soup.

Okra: Ideal for pickling or freezing.

Spinach: Appropriate for whitening and freezing or making spinach puree for sauces.

Make sure to follow appropriate protection techniques to guarantee the best quality and well-being of your safeguarded vegetables.

Washing and Cleaning

Washing and cleaning vegetables is fundamental for protection. Here are a few stages:

Begin by cleaning up completely.

Utilize perfect, cold water to wash the vegetables.

Tenderly clean them with a brush or your hands to eliminate soil flotsam and jetsam.

For mixed greens, separate the leaves and absorb them in a bowl of cold water. Wash them around to eliminate any soil or bugs.

Utilize a vinegar-water arrangement (1 section vinegar to 3 sections water) to splash the vegetables for a couple of moments. This can assist with eliminating microbes and pesticides.

Flush the vegetables again with clean water to eliminate any excess vinegar.

Dry them with a perfect kitchen towel or paper towel.

Store in impenetrable holders or resealable sacks in the cooler to draw out newness.

For root vegetables like carrots and potatoes, utilize a vegetable brush to scour off soil, however, try not to strip them, as the skin helps save newness and supplements.

Eliminate any withered or harmed pieces of the vegetables before cleaning to keep decay from spreading.

Mixed greens like lettuce and kale ought to be dried completely utilizing a plate of mixed greens spinner or by tapping them delicately with a spotless kitchen towel to forestall overabundance dampness, which can prompt decay.

Abstain from washing mushrooms under running water; all things considered, utilize a moist paper towel or a mushroom brush to eliminate soil and clean them.

For sensitive spices, trim the stems and spot them in a glass of water, covering the leaves with a plastic sack, and storing them in the cooler to keep them new for longer.

Make certain to wash vegetables regardless of whether you intend to strip them, as cutting into unwashed produce can move soil and microorganisms to the edible part.

Keep your cooler's vegetable crisper cabinet spotless and dry, as dampness and soil in the cabinet can speed up vegetable waste.

Store various vegetables independently, as some delivery gasses can influence others. For instance, keep ethylene-delivering vegetables like tomatoes from ethylene-touchy ones like mixed greens.

Utilize a food-safe sanitizer while cleaning hard-cleaned vegetables like melons, squash, and cucumbers to dispose of expected pollutants on a superficial level.

Occasionally check put away vegetables for indications of waste and eliminate any that have turned sour to forestall the spread of rot.

Following these tips will assist with guaranteeing your vegetables stay new and alright for longer periods, diminishing food waste, and setting aside your cash.

Cutting and Slicing Techniques

Safeguarding vegetables through cutting and cutting strategies can assist with broadening their period of usability. Here are a few normal techniques:

Freezing: Cut or cut the vegetables into wanted sizes, whiten them momentarily in bubbling water, and then, at that point, immediately cool them in ice water before freezing. This holds the surface and flavor.

Drying out: Cut vegetables meagerly and get dried out utilizing a food dehydrator or a broiler at a low temperature. Dried-out vegetables can be put away for a lengthy period.

Pickling: Cutting vegetables like cucumbers, carrots, or onions and lowering them in a brackish water or vinegar arrangement can protect them for a significant time frame.

Canning: Cut vegetables into reasonable pieces, then put them in containers with legitimate canning at any point cycle, including heat treatment to kill microbes and catalysts that can cause waste.

Maturation: Cut vegetables and age them with salt, making items like sauerkraut or kimchi, which can be put away for quite a long time in the right circumstances.

Salting: A few vegetables can be saved by cutting and layering them with salt, which draws out dampness and goes about as an additive. This is normal for things like salted cabbage.

Oil protection: Cutting vegetables and putting away them in oil can assist with safeguarding their flavor and surface. This is frequently utilized for things like sun-dried tomatoes in olive oil.

Root Basement Stockpiling: Some root vegetables like potatoes, carrots, and beets can be cut or put away entirely in a cool, dim root basement to draw out their timeframe of realistic usability.

Whiten and Refrigerate: In the wake of whitening, you can store cut vegetables in the cooler for a more limited-term protection technique. They'll remain new for a couple of days to a long time.

Vacuum Fixing: Utilizing a vacuum sealer, you can cut vegetables into reasonable divides and vacuum-seal them in plastic packs. This strategy eliminates air, forestalling oxidation, and deterioration.

Implanted Vinegar: Cut or dice vegetables like garlic, stew peppers, or spices and spot them in vinegar. This makes seasoned vinegar that can be utilized for cooking and protection.

Sun-Drying: Cutting vegetables meagerly and sun-drying them is a conventional protection strategy. This functions admirably for things like sun-dried tomatoes and can be put away in hermetically sealed compartments.

Tenderizing: Lower vegetables like cucumbers, green beans, or peppers in a saltwater brackish water arrangement. This strategy is utilized for making pickles and other tenderized vegetables.

Purée and Freeze: Mix vegetables like tomatoes or peppers into a purée, then freeze them in segments. This is perfect for making sauces and soups.

Spice Margarine: Blend cut spices into relaxed spread, then freeze in segments. This spice margarine can be utilized to enhance dishes.

Dry Powder: Drudgery dried, cut vegetables into powder, for example, garlic or onion powder. Store in hermetically sealed compartments for a more extended timeframe of realistic usability.

Spice 3D squares: Cut spices can be frozen in an ice block plate with water, making spice-implanted ice shapes that can be added to cook.

Recall that the decision of method relies upon the kind of vegetable and your planned use. Furthermore, appropriate capacity holders and marking are fundamental for a coordinated and effective safeguarding process.

Blanching for Optimal Flavor and Color

Whitening is a significant stage in vegetable conservation. It includes momentarily submerging vegetables in bubbling water, trailed by fast cooling in ice water. This cycle fills a few needs:

Chemical deactivation: Whitening stops enzymatic responses that can cause loss of flavor, variety, and supplements in vegetables over the long haul.

Variety maintenance: Whitening helps save the lively shades of vegetables by annihilating chemicals that cause staining.

Flavor safeguarding: It secures the new kind of vegetables and can further develop their taste when appropriately finished.

Cleanliness and well-being: Whitening likewise helps in cleaning and disinfecting the vegetables.

Pick new vegetables: Begin with superior grade, new vegetables for the best outcomes in protecting flavor and variety.

Wash and clean: Completely wash the vegetables before whitening to eliminate any soil or pollutants.

Utilize the right gear: Utilize a huge pot for whitening to guarantee in any event, cooking and keep up with water temperature. A whitening bin or a wire network sifter is likewise helpful.

Bubbling water: Utilize a huge volume of overwhelmingly bubbling water, regularly 1 gallon (4 liters) per pound of vegetables.

Salt (discretionary): Adding a limited quantity of salt to the whitening water can improve the kind of certain vegetables, yet all the same it's discretionary.

Bunch size: Don't stuff the whitening pot; whiten in little clusters to keep a fast bubble.

Whitening times: Various vegetables have fluctuating whitening times. Allude to a dependable hotspot for explicit times.

Cooling time: Quickly move whitened vegetables to ice water to cool. This stops the cooking system and secures the variety and flavor.

Ice water shower: Guarantee the ice water shower is to some degree as cold as 40°F (4°C) to cool the vegetables rapidly.

Channel completely: In the wake of cooling, channel the vegetables well to forestall abundance dampness in your conservation technique.

Bundling for freezing: On the off chance that you intend to freeze whitened vegetables, bundle them in sealed shut holders or cooler packs, eliminating however much air as could reasonably be expected to forestall cooler consumption.

Mark and date: Consistently name and date your saved vegetables to monitor newness.

Utilize a whitening graph: Counsel a whitening diagram or guide for explicit whitening times for various vegetables.

Consider whitening options: While bubbling is the most widely recognized strategy, a few vegetables can be whitened by steam or microwave.

Try and get the hang of: Whitening might require experimentation to obtain the ideal outcomes, so make it a point to investigate and tweak your method.

Recall that whitening is a basic move toward safeguarding vegetables, and when done accurately, it can assist with keeping up with their quality, flavor, and variety for a lengthy period.

Chapter 2: Basic Canning Methods

Water Bath Canning

Water shower canning is a food safeguarding strategy used to handle high-corrosive food varieties like natural products, sticks, and pickles. It includes fixing containers of arranged food in a bubbling water shower to make a vacuum seal and forestalling decay. Assuming you have explicit inquiries concerning water shower canning, go ahead and inquire!

Water shower canning is principally utilized for high-corrosive food sources, like natural products, sticks, and pickles. For low-corrosive food sources like vegetables, you ought to utilize a strain canner for safe conservation. Be that as it may, here are a few normal strategies for protecting vegetables:

Pressure Canning: This strategy is fundamental for low-corrosive vegetables like green beans, carrots, and corn. Pressure canners use steam strain to kill harmful microorganisms. Follow a confided-in recipe and canning guide for exact directions.

Freezing: Numerous vegetables can be whitened (momentarily bubbled) and afterward frozen for longer-term capacity. Freezing keeps up with the nature of the produce however doesn't kill microorganisms and catalysts like canning does.

Pickling: Vegetables like cucumbers, peppers, and onions can be safeguarded by pickling in vinegar and flavors. You can utilize a water shower canner to seal the containers if the recipe is determined.

Drying: Getting dried-out vegetables eliminates dampness and forestalling deterioration. You can utilize a food dehydrator or stove for this strategy.

Maturation: Aging vegetables, similar to sauerkraut and kimchi, is a characteristic conservation technique that upgrades flavor and adds probiotics. It doesn't include canning, yet it broadens the timeframe of realistic usability.

Water shower canning is normally not suggested for protecting low-corrosive vegetables because of the gamble of botulism. Nonetheless, if you need to make cured vegetables for transient use (refrigeration expected), here's a fundamental recipe:

Cured Vegetables:

Fixings:

New vegetables (e.g., cucumbers, carrots, cauliflower, chime peppers)

Pickling fluid (a balance of water and vinegar, normally white or juice vinegar)

Salt

Sugar

Flavors (e.g., garlic, dill, mustard seeds, red pepper drops)

Guidelines:

Wash and set up your vegetables. Cut them into wanted sizes and pack them into cleaned canning containers.

In a pan, join a balance of water and vinegar (e.g., 1 cup of each). Add 1-2 tablespoons of salt and sugar to taste. Heat the blend to the point of boiling.

Add flavors to the containers with the vegetables. Normal increments incorporate garlic cloves, dill, mustard seeds, and a touch of red pepper drops for heat.

Empty the hot pickling fluid into the containers, leaving around 1/2 inch of headspace at the top. Utilize an air pocket remover instrument to deliver air bubbles, then change the fluid level if necessary.

Wipe the container edges to guarantee they're perfect and put disinfected covers and groups on the containers. Seal them firmly.

Process the containers in a bubbling water shower for around 10-15 minutes. The water ought to cover the containers by basically an inch.

Eliminate the containers and let them cool. Look at the seals after cooling; the covers ought to be inward and not flex when squeezed.

Store the fixed containers in the cooler for momentary use. Appropriately fixed containers can be put away at cool room temperature for a considerable length of time.

Keep in mind that this technique is for cured vegetables to be consumed generally rapidly and kept in the ice chest. For long-haul stockpiling of low-corrosive vegetables, utilize a strain canner following a safe canning methodology.

Pressure Canning

Pressure canning is a protected technique for saving vegetables. It includes utilizing a strain canner to handle vegetables at a high temperature and tension, which assists with obliterating unsafe microorganisms like botulism spores. Here are the fundamental stages for pressure canning vegetables:

Set up your vegetables by washing, stripping, and cutting them depending on the situation.

Fill clean canning containers with the pre-arranged vegetables, leaving the suggested headspace (regularly 1 inch) at the highest point of the container.

Add heated water or a reasonable fluid, similar to stock, to the containers, leaving the suggested headspace.

Wipe the container edges clean and put the covers and screw groups on the containers.

Place the filled containers in the strain canner, adhering to the maker's directions for water level and venting.

Process the containers at the suitable strain and time for your particular vegetables and elevation. Allude to a dependable canning guide for this data.

When handling is finished, switch off the intensity, permit the canner to decompress, and trust that the tension will get back to business as usual.

Cautiously eliminate the containers from the canner and put them on a spotless, dry surface.

Allow the containers to cool, and guarantee the covers have been fixed appropriately by checking for a vacuum seal (a popping sound when pushed down on the focal point of the top).

Name and store the fixed containers in a cool, dim, and dry spot.

It's essential to follow legitimate canning methods and utilize tried recipes to guarantee the security of your saved vegetables. On the off chance that you're new to pressure canning, counsel a legitimate canning guide or nearby expansion office for direction on unambiguous vegetables and elevation changes.

Here is an essential recipe for pressure canning green beans:

Pressure Canned Green Beans:

Fixings:

New green beans

Water

Canning salt (discretionary, for some character)

Hardware:

Pressure canner

Canning containers, tops, and screw groups

Container lifter

Canning channel

Enormous pot for whitening

Guidelines:

Set up Your Hardware:

Wash and sanitize canning containers, tops, and screw groups.

Check your strain canner to guarantee it's in great working condition.

Set up the Green Beans:

Wash the green beans completely.

Trim the closures and slice them into 1 to 2-inch pieces or leave them entire, as wanted.

Whiten the Green Beans:

Fill a huge pot with water and heat it to the point of boiling.

Add the green beans to the bubbling water and whiten them for 2-3 minutes.

Immediately move the whitened beans to a bowl of ice water to stop the cooking system.

Channel the beans.

Fill the Containers:

Utilizing a canning pipe, pack the whitened green beans into the disinfected canning containers, leaving around 1 inch of headspace.

Whenever wanted, add 1/2 teaspoon of canning salt to every 16-ounce container (adapt to quart containers).

Add Water:

Fill each container with high-temperature water, leaving 1 inch of headspace.

Eliminate Air pockets:

Embed a spotless utensil or air pocket remover device into the containers to deliver any caught air.

Wipe Container Edges:

Clean the container edges with a spotless, moist fabric to guarantee a decent seal.

Secure Tops and Groups:

Put sanitized tops and screw groups on the containers, adhering to the maker's directions for fixing.

Tension Can:

Adhere to the strain canner producer's directions for adding water and venting.

Process the containers at the suitable tension for your height and green beans (ordinarily around 10-11 pounds of strain for 20-25 minutes for half-quart containers).

Keep up with the tension and handling time as suggested.

Cool and Store:

In the wake of handling, switch off the intensity and let the canner decompress normally.

Cautiously eliminate the containers and put them on a spotless towel or cooling rack.

Allow the containers to cool totally, and take a look at the seals.

Name the fixed containers with the date and store them in a cool, dull, and dry spot.

Kindly note that handling times and tension might fluctuate depending on your area and the particular canning rules for your green beans. Continuously counsel a solid canning asset or your nearby expansion office for exact proposals.

Steam Canning

Steam canning isn't suggested for saving vegetables since it may not give the essential intensity to kill unsafe microorganisms and catalysts in vegetables. All things considered, water shower canning or pressure canning is by and large suggested for saving vegetables securely.

Here is a fundamental cycle for water shower canning vegetables:

Select new vegetables and wash them completely.

Set up the canning containers and tops by cleaning them.

Whiten the vegetables in bubbling water for a brief time frame (generally a couple of moments) to safeguard the tone and surface.

Pack the hot vegetables into the cleaned containers, leaving the proper headspace as suggested for your particular vegetable.

Fill the containers with a saline solution or water, they are completely covered to guarantee the vegetables.

Eliminate air rises by running a non-metallic utensil around within the container.

Wipe the container edges, put tops and screw groups on the containers, and seal them.

Process the containers in a bubbling water shower for the suggested time given the particular vegetable and your height.

Eliminate the containers, let them cool, and check for appropriate fixing...

The following are two exemplary vegetable canning recipes for cured cucumbers and canned tomatoes:

Salted Cucumbers (Dill Pickles):

Fixings:

4-5 pounds of pickling cucumbers

2 1/2 cups white vinegar (5% causticity)

2 1/2 cups water

1/4 cup pickling salt

2-3 cloves of garlic for every container

New dill branches

Entire dark peppercorns

Mustard seeds (discretionary)

Grape leaves (discretionary, for freshness)

Guidelines:

Disinfect canning containers and covers.

Wash the cucumbers and trim off the bloom.

In an enormous pot, consolidate vinegar, water, and pickling salt. Heat to the point of boiling to make the brackish water.

Load each cleaned container with garlic cloves, new dill, dark peppercorns, and other discretionary flavors.

Pack the cucumbers into the containers firmly, leaving around 1/2 inch of headspace.

Pour the hot brackish water over the cucumbers, leaving 1/4 inch of headspace.

Eliminate air bubbles, wipe the container edges, put sanitized tops and screw groups on the containers, and seal.

Process the containers in a bubbling water shower for around 10-15 minutes, contingent on your height.

Eliminate the containers, let them cool, and guarantee they seal appropriately.

Canned Tomatoes:

Fixings:

Ready tomatoes

Lemon juice or citrus extract (for causticity, see suggested sums for your height)

Salt (discretionary)

Directions:

Clean canning containers and tops.

Wash the tomatoes and whiten them in bubbling water for around 30 seconds, then move to an ice water shower to effortlessly strip.

Eliminate the centers and any flaws from the tomatoes.

Pack the stripped and cored tomatoes into cleaned containers, leaving around 1/2 inch of headspace.

Add lemon juice or citrus extract to each container keeping the suggested rules for corrosiveness.

You can add a touch of salt whenever you want.

Eliminate air bubbles, wipe the container edges, put cleaned tops and screw groups on the containers, and seal.

Process the containers in a bubbling water shower for the suggested time for your height.

Eliminate the containers, let them cool, and guarantee they seal appropriately.

If it's not too much trouble, note that these are fundamental recipes, and you ought to constantly observe explicit canning rules for your elevation and counsel confided in hotspots for additional definite directions to guarantee security and quality in your canning cycle.

Altitude Adjustments for Canning

Height can influence the limit of water, which, thus, can affect the canning system for safeguarding vegetables. At higher heights, water bubbles at lower temperatures because of the lower climatic tension. To adapt to height while canning vegetables:

Counsel a dependable canning guide or recipe: Consistently start with a trusted canning asset, for example, the USDA Complete Manual for Home Canning, or the Ball Blue Book Manual for Safeguarding. These sources frequently give elevation acclimations to explicit recipes.

Change handling times: Generally speaking, you'll have to build the handling time while canning at higher elevations. This makes up for the lower edge of boiling over water and guarantees that the vegetables are securely protected. Allude to your canning guide for suggested time changes.

Keep up with legitimate tension: On the off chance that you're utilizing a strain canner, you'll have to change the strain setting as per your elevation. Higher heights require higher strain to accomplish the important temperature for safe canning. Check your canner's manual or the canning guide for explicit strain changes.

Utilize a thermometer: It's a decent practice to utilize a thermometer to screen the temperature of your canner. This guarantees that you reach and keep up with the right temperature for your height.

Follow suggested canning rehearses: Consistently utilize spotless, sterile containers and covers, and follow the suggested systems for canning, like headspace, pre-handling planning, and cooling.

Test your height: To decide the right changes for your particular elevation, you can utilize a height-adding machine or reference neighborhood assets. It's essential to be all around as precise as possible to guarantee safe conservation.

Recall that protected canning rehearses are critical for forestalling foodborne diseases. Following height changes, handling times, and suggested rules from believed sources is fundamental to guaranteeing the well-being and nature of your canned vegetables.

, here are a few extra subtleties on elevation changes for canning vegetables:

Figure out height classifications: Elevation changes are regularly made given height classes. The classes are frequently characterized as follows:

Ocean level to 1,000 feet (0-305 meters): Low height

1,001 to 3,000 feet (306-914 meters): Medium height

3,001 to 6,000 feet (915-1,828 meters): High height

Over 6,000 feet (1,829 meters): Exceptionally high elevation

Factors influencing height changes: Elevation changes are vital because the lower barometrical strain at higher elevations brings about a lower edge of boiling over water. This influences the temperature at which your canned vegetables need to go for safe protection. At higher heights, the handling time or tension should be expanded to make up for the lower edge of boiling over.

Utilizing a height diagram: Many canning assets give elevation graphs that indicate the changes expected for various heights. These graphs will demonstrate the suggested handling time or tension setting for every height classification.

Wellbeing first: Consistently focus on security while canning. Utilizing a tension canner is particularly significant for low-corrosive vegetables like green beans, as killing potential botulism spores is fundamental. Guarantee your canner is ready to go, the seals are flawless, and you're following all well-being precautionary measures.

Be exact: Precise elevation estimations are essential for making the right changes. You can decide your precise height utilizing a GPS gadget, a geographical guide, or a web-based device, as even little contrasts in elevation can affect the canning system.

Test for seal respectability: In the wake of canning look at the seals on your containers to guarantee they are appropriately fixed. Push down on the focal point of the cover; it shouldn't flex or make a popping sound. This demonstrates a fruitful seal. If a container doesn't seal, refrigerate its items and use them quickly or go back over the container.

By adhering to these extra tips and rules, you can with certainty change your canning interaction to represent height and guarantee the protected safeguarding of your vegetables. Continuously depend on legitimate canning assets and neighborhood height data for precise changes.

Chapter 3: Prickling Vegetables

Dill Pickles

Dill pickles are a sort of salted cucumber regularly seasoned with dill weed and garlic. They're a famous bite and fixing known for their tart and exquisite flavor.

Fixings: To make dill pickles, you'll require cucumbers, new dill, garlic cloves, white vinegar, water, salt, and discretionary flavors like dark peppercorns, mustard seeds, or red pepper chips.

Saline solution: The brackish water is a combination of water, vinegar, and salt. It's warmed and afterward poured over the cucumbers and flavors.

Readiness: Begin by washing and cutting the cucumbers. Place them in a disinfected container or compartment alongside new dill and garlic cloves.

Heating the Saline solution: In a pot, consolidate water, vinegar, and salt. Heat it to the point of boiling, then let it stew for a couple of moments to guarantee the salt is broken down.

Pouring the Brackish water: When the saline solution is prepared, cautiously pour it over the cucumbers in the container. Ensure the cucumbers are completely lowered in the salt water.

Cooling and Fixing: Permit the pickles to cool at room temperature, then seal the container with a top and refrigerate it. They will require a chance to foster their flavor, generally a couple of days to seven days.

Varieties: You can try different things with various flavors and spices in your dill pickles. Certain individuals like to add inlet leaves, coriander seeds, or even a hint of sugar for a better note.

Capacity: Store your hand-crafted dill pickles in the fridge. They will save for a long time to a couple of months.

Happiness: Dill pickles make an extraordinary nibble all alone, or you can involve them as a topping for sandwiches, burgers, or as a side dish with different feasts.

Natively constructed dill pickles can be a tomfoolery and scrumptious task, permitting you to modify the flavor however you would prefer.

Here is an essential recipe for natively constructed dill pickles:

Fixings:

4-6 pickling cucumbers

2-3 new dill twigs

2-3 cloves of garlic, stripped and cut

1 cup white vinegar

1 cup water

1 1/2 tablespoons legitimate salt

Discretionary flavors: dark peppercorns, mustard seeds, red pepper chips

Directions:

Set up the Cucumbers: Wash the cucumbers completely and cut off the finishes. You can leave them entire or cut them into lances or cuts, contingent upon your inclination.

Set up the Container: Clean a glass container or holder by running it through a dishwasher or lowering it in bubbling water for a couple of moments. Guarantee it's spotless and dry.

Add Flavors: Spot the new dill branches and cut garlic at the lower part of the cleaned container. You can likewise add any discretionary flavors you like at this stage.

Pack the Cucumbers: Pack the pre-arranged cucumbers firmly into the container, leaving about an inch of room at the top.

Make the Saline solution: In a pot, consolidate the white vinegar, water, and genuine salt. Heat the combination over medium-high intensity, blending until the salt is completely broken up. Eliminate from heat once it begins to bubble.

Pour the Saltwater: Cautiously pour the hot saline solution over the cucumbers in the container, it is completely lowered to guarantee they. Leave around 1/2 inch of room at the top.

Seal the Container: Put a cover on the container and screw it on firmly. Allow the container to cool to room temperature.

Refrigerate: When the container has cooled, place it in the cooler. The pickles will begin to foster their flavor following a little while.

Pause and Appreciate: Permit the pickles to sit in the cooler for essentially a couple of days, preferably possibly more than seven days, for the best character. The more they sit, the more serious the dill pickle flavor will turn into.

Serve: Partake in your hand-crafted dill pickles as a tidbit, on sandwiches, or as a side dish with your number one feast.

Go ahead and change the recipe as you would prefer by adding pretty much garlic, dill, or flavors. Custom-made dill pickles can be a wonderful expansion to your culinary manifestations.

Bread and Butter Pickles

Bread and butter pickles are a sort of sweet and tart pickle produced using cucumbers, onions, and a combination of sugar, vinegar, and flavors. They are a famous sauce in the US and are frequently utilized on sandwiches or as a side dish.

Sweet and Tart Flavor: Bread and butter pickles are known for their sweet and tart flavor profile, which makes them a number one among individuals who partake in an equilibrium of prepared in their pickles.

Cut Cucumbers: These pickles are commonly made with meagerly cut cucumbers, which are marinated in the sugar and vinegar brackish water alongside cut onions.

Extraordinary for Sandwiches: Bread and butter pickles are in many cases utilized as a fixing for sandwiches, particularly for things like cheeseburgers, wieners, and store sandwiches.

Natively constructed Versus Locally acquired: You can find bread and butter pickles in most supermarkets, however many individuals likewise appreciate making them at home, as hand-crafted adaptations can be redone to suit individual inclinations.

Canning and Safeguarding: These pickles can be canned or bumped, permitting them to be put away for a drawn-out period. This goes with their well-known decision to protect the mid-year cucumber reap.

Fixings: The vital fixings in meat and potato pickles normally incorporate cucumbers, onions, sugar, white vinegar, mustard seeds, celery seeds, and turmeric.

Varieties: While the exemplary rendition is made with cucumbers, a few varieties utilize different vegetables like zucchini or even a blend of vegetables for a novel curve.

Tidbit and Starter: Bread and butter pickles can likewise be delighted in as a delicious bite or hors d'oeuvre all alone.

Provincial Varieties: Various locales in the US might have their varieties of meat and potato pickles, with slight contrasts in flavor and fixings.

Flexibility: These pickles can add a sweet and tart kick to different dishes, from plates of mixed greens to potato servings of mixed greens and then some.

Is there anything explicit you might want to be aware of or examine about meat and potato pickles?

here is an essential recipe for making custom-made bread and butter pickles:

Fixings:

4-5 cups of daintily cut cucumbers

1 cup of daintily cut onions

1/4 cup of canning salt

2 cups of white sugar

1 cup of white vinegar

1/2 cup of apple juice vinegar

2 tablespoons of mustard seeds

1/2 teaspoon of celery seeds

1/4 teaspoon of ground turmeric

Directions:

Start by cutting the cucumbers and onions daintily. You can utilize a mandoline slicer for uniform cuts.

In an enormous blending bowl, consolidate the cut cucumbers, onions, and canning salt. Throw them together, cover them, and allow them to sit for around 2 hours. This will draw out the overabundance of dampness from the vegetables.

For 2 hours, wash the cucumbers and onions completely under cool water to eliminate the salt. Channel well and put away.

In an enormous pot, join the white sugar, white vinegar, apple juice vinegar, mustard seeds, celery seeds, and ground turmeric. Heat the blend to the point of boiling, mixing until the sugar is broken up.

Add the depleted cucumbers and onions to the bubbling saline solution blend. Mix well and let it come to a delicate stew. Permit it to stew for around 5 minutes, or until the cucumbers simply start to turn clear.

Eliminate the pot from the intensity. Your meat and potatoes pickles are presently fit to be canned or jolted. You can follow appropriate canning systems to protect them for long-haul stockpiling.

On the off chance that you don't want to can them, you can store the pickles in a hermetically sealed compartment in the cooler for half a month. They will foster more flavor as they sit.

This is an essential recipe, and you can change the pleasantness, tartness, or heat as you would prefer. Partake in your natively constructed bread and butter pickles on sandwiches or as a delicious sauce!

Pickled Peppers

To pickle peppers, you can follow these general advances:

Pick your peppers: Select new, firm peppers of your decision, for example, jalapeños, chime peppers, or banana peppers. You can involve a blend for assortment.

Wash and cut: Wash the peppers and afterward cut them into your ideal shape, like rings, strips, or entire if they are little.

Plan saline solution: In a pan, consolidate equivalent pieces of water and vinegar (normally white vinegar), and add sugar and salt to taste. You can likewise incorporate different flavors like garlic, peppercorns, or spices for added character.

Heat to the point of boiling: Intensity the saline solution over medium intensity, mixing until the sugar and salt break up. When it reaches boiling point, eliminate it from the intensity and let it cool somewhat.

Pack the peppers: Spot the cut peppers into disinfected glass containers, leaving some space at the top. Pour the salt water over the peppers to cover them.

Seal the containers: Guarantee the containers are appropriately fixed. You can get canning tops and rings for this reason.

Store: Permit the salted peppers to cool at room temperature and afterward store them in the fridge for a couple of days to allow the flavors to create. They will be prepared to eat in about seven days.

Appreciate: Salted peppers can be utilized as a fixing, in sandwiches, mixed greens, or as a delicious expansion to different dishes.

Make sure to observe legitimate sanitation rules while pickling to guarantee your cured peppers stay protected to eat.

The following are a couple of additional pickling recipes for you to attempt:

Cured Cucumbers (Dill Pickles):

Fixings: Cucumbers, new dill, garlic cloves, white vinegar, water, salt, sugar, and dark peppercorns.

Directions: Cut cucumbers into lances or adjusts. In a container, layer cucumbers, dill, and garlic. Bring a combination of vinegar, water, salt, sugar, and peppercorns to a bubble, then pour it over the cucumbers. Seal and refrigerate for a couple of days.

Salted Red Onions:

Fixings: Red onions, apple juice vinegar, water, sugar, salt, and dark peppercorns.

Guidelines: Cut red onions daintily. In a pan, consolidate vinegar, water, sugar, salt, and peppercorns. Heat until the sugar breaks down. Pour the combination over the onions in a container and refrigerate for a couple of hours before utilizing.

Salted Beets:

Fixings: Beets, apple juice vinegar, water, sugar, salt, and entire cloves.

Guidelines: Cook beets until delicate, then, at that point, strip and cut them. In a pot, combine vinegar, water, sugar, salt, and cloves. Heat until sugar breaks up. Place beets in a container and pour the fluid over them. Seal and refrigerate for a couple of days.

Cured Carrots:

Fixings: Carrots, white vinegar, water, sugar, salt, coriander seeds, and sound leaves.

Directions: Cut or julienne carrots. In a pot, combine vinegar, water, sugar, salt, coriander seeds, and narrow leaves. Heat until sugar breaks up. Place carrots in a container and pour the fluid over them. Seal and refrigerate for a couple of days.

These recipes offer various salted choices, and you can change the flavors and flavors to suit your taste inclinations. Appreciate exploring different avenues regarding various vegetables and flavors!

Pickled Green Tomatoes

Pickling green tomatoes is an extraordinary method for saving them and partaking in their tart flavor. Here is a fundamental recipe for cured green tomatoes:

Fixings:

Green tomatoes

Vinegar (white or apple juice vinegar)

Water

Pickling salt (non-iodized)

Sugar

Pickling flavors (discretionary, you can utilize a blend of mustard seeds, coriander, dill seeds, and red pepper pieces)

Guidelines:

Wash the green tomatoes completely and cut them into rounds or wedges. You can likewise leave them entire assuming that they are little.

In a huge pot, join a balance of water and vinegar. For the saline solution, you can utilize a proportion of 1:1 water to vinegar, and change the sum contingent upon the quantity of tomatoes you have.

Add pickling salt and sugar to the saline solution. Normally, for each 1 cup of vinegar-water combination, you can add 1-2 tablespoons of salt and 1-2 tablespoons of sugar. Change per your taste.

Assuming that you like, add pickling flavors to the saline solution to upgrade the flavor. You can use around 1-2 tablespoons of blended flavors per cup of saline solution.

Heat the saline solution to the point of boiling and afterward decrease the intensity to a stew for a couple of moments.

Place the green tomato cuts or entire tomatoes into perfect, disinfected containers.

Pour the hot salt water over the tomatoes in the containers, leaving around 1/2 inch of headspace at the top.

Wipe the container edges clean, put disinfected tops and groups on the containers, and seal them firmly.

Process the fixed containers in a bubbling water shower for around 10-15 minutes to guarantee they are appropriately fixed and saved. The specific handling time might change because of your height, so counsel canning rules for your area.

Allow the cured green tomatoes to cool to room temperature, and store them in a cool, dim spot for a long time before opening to permit the flavors to be created.

After the cured green tomatoes have developed for half a month, you can appreciate them as a tasty and tart sauce or bite. Make certain to take a look at the seals on your containers to guarantee they're okay for utilization.

Fermented pickles and kimchi

Pickling green tomatoes is an extraordinary method for saving them and partaking in their tart flavor. Here is a fundamental recipe for cured green tomatoes:

Fixings:

Green tomatoes

Vinegar (white or apple juice vinegar)

Water

Pickling salt (non-iodized)

Sugar

Pickling flavors (discretionary, you can utilize a blend of mustard seeds, coriander, dill seeds, and red pepper pieces)

Guidelines:

Wash the green tomatoes completely and cut them into rounds or wedges. You can likewise leave them entire assuming that they are little.

In a huge pot, join a balance of water and vinegar. For the saline solution, you can utilize a proportion of 1:1 water to vinegar, and change the sum contingent upon the quantity of tomatoes you have.

Add pickling salt and sugar to the saline solution. Normally, for each 1 cup of vinegar-water combination, you can add 1-2 tablespoons of salt and 1-2 tablespoons of sugar. Change per your taste.

Assuming that you like, add pickling flavors to the saline solution to upgrade the flavor. You can use around 1-2 tablespoons of blended flavors per cup of saline solution.

Heat the saline solution to the point of boiling and afterward decrease the intensity to a stew for a couple of moments.

Place the green tomato cuts or entire tomatoes into perfect, disinfected containers.

Pour the hot salt water over the tomatoes in the containers, leaving around 1/2 inch of headspace at the top.

Wipe the container edges clean, put disinfected tops and groups on the containers, and seal them firmly.

Process the fixed containers in a bubbling water shower for around 10-15 minutes to guarantee they are appropriately fixed and saved. The specific handling time might change because of your height, so counsel canning rules for your area.

Allow the cured green tomatoes to cool to room temperature, and store them in a cool, dim spot for a long time before opening to permit the flavors to be created.

After the cured green tomatoes have developed for half a month, you can appreciate them as a tasty and tart sauce or bite. Make certain to take a look at the seals on your containers to guarantee they're okay for utilization.

Sweet and Savory Pickling Solutions

Sweet and impeccable pickling game plans are used to safeguard and improve different food sources. A fundamental sweet pickling game plan routinely contains sugar, water, and vinegar, while a tasty one could integrate trimmings like salt, flavors, and garlic. You can make different relieved things, from sweet bread and butter pickles to choice dill pickles or salted onions, by changing the trimmings and extents to achieve your optimal taste.

Certainly! Pickling game plans, generally called pickling saline arrangements, are the liquid mixes used to shield and flavor food assortments through pickling. Here is a few additional information about sweet and mouth-watering pickling plans:

Sweet Pickling Course of action:

Basic Trimmings: A sweet pickling game plan usually contains sugar, water, and vinegar. The sugar gives enjoyableness, while vinegar adds causticity for assurance.

Flavorings: Sweet pickles often consolidate flavorings like mustard seeds, celery seeds, and turmeric. These flavors overhaul the taste.

Tasty Pickling Game plan:

Fundamental Trimmings: Appealing pickling game plans contain water, vinegar, salt, and flavors. Salt is pressing for cajoling sogginess out of the food and safeguarding it.

Flavorings: Ordinary flavors in flawless pickles consolidate dill, garlic, dim peppercorns, coriander seeds, and bay leaves. These flavors give the pickles a more dazzling and sharp flavor.

Changing the Harmony:

The extent of sugar to vinegar in sweet pickles can be accustomed to achieve the best level of agreeableness. A couple of recipes furthermore use elective sugars like honey or maple syrup.

In wonderful pickles, the sort and proportion of flavors can be revamped to make different flavor profiles. You can investigate various roads in regards to blends to suit your taste.

Food Sources You Can Pickle:

Sweet pickles are oftentimes used for cucumbers, beets, and normal items like peaches and pears.

Dazzling pickles are ideal for cucumbers (dill pickles), onions, carrots, and anything is possible from that point. They are also used for matured things like sauerkraut and kimchi.

Pickling Collaboration:

The pickling framework remembers bringing down the nourishment for the pickling game plan and allowing it to sit for some time to hold the flavors. The time frame varies depending on the food and recipe.

Recall that the specific recipes and extents for sweet and delightful pickling plans can vacillate, so it's an issue of individual tendency. The result is luscious, safeguarded food assortments with fascinating and incredible flavors. Is there whatever unequivocal you could need to know or any recipes you're enthusiastic about?

Here are key recipes for both sweet and delightful pickling game plans, as well as a recipe for salted cucumbers (an excellent decision):

Fundamental Sweet Pickling Plan:

Trimmings:

2 cups white vinegar

1 1/2 cups granulated sugar

2 cups water

1 tablespoon mustard seeds

1/2 teaspoon celery seeds

1/2 teaspoon turmeric

Bearings:

In a skillet, combine vinegar, sugar, water, mustard seeds, celery seeds, and turmeric. Heat the blend with the eventual result of bubbling, then, diminish the power and stew until the sugar is separated.

Let the sweet pickling game plan cool to room temperature preceding including it for pickling.

Key Lovely Pickling Game plan:

Trimmings:

2 cups white vinegar

2 cups water

2 tablespoons salt

2 cloves garlic, squashed

1 tablespoon dill seeds

1 teaspoon dull peppercorns

2 inlet leaves

Rules:

In a dish, combine vinegar, water, salt, garlic, dill seeds, dull peppercorns, and strait leaves. Heat the blend with the result of bubbling, then kill it from heat.

Grant the tempting pickling reply for cool to room temperature before including it for pickling.

Salted Cucumbers (Dill Pickles):

Trimmings:

4-6 pickling cucumbers

2-3 parts of new dill (or 2 teaspoons dill seeds)

2 cloves garlic, stripped

1/2 teaspoon dim peppercorns

1/4 teaspoon red pepper drops (optional for heat)

1 quart-sized glass holder with a top

Rules:

Wash the cucumbers and cut off the sprout end (the end contains the stem).

Place the dill, garlic, dim peppercorns, and red pepper pieces (if using) in the lower part of the glass compartment.

Pack the cucumbers into the holder immovably, leaving around 1/2 inch of room at the top.

Pour the tantalizing pickling game plan over the cucumbers, ensuring they are brought down.

Seal the holder with a cover and store it in the ice chest for somewhere in the ballpark of 24 hours preceding participating in your grasp-created dill pickles.

These are fundamental recipes to start you off. You can change the trimmings and degrees to suit your taste. Lively pickling!

Chapter 4: Jams, Jellies, and Chutneys

Tomato Jam

Tomato jam is a topping or save produced using tomatoes, sugar, and different flavors. It's like natural product sticks or jams however is made utilizing ready tomatoes. The tomatoes are normally cooked down with sugar, vinegar, and flavorings like flavors or spices to make a sweet and exquisite spread. Tomato jam can be utilized as a garnish for sandwiches, burgers, or cheddar, or as a sauce to add a one-of-a-kind flavor to different dishes.

Flavor Profile: Tomato jam has a special sweet and exquisite flavor with a touch of corrosiveness from the tomatoes. The sugar adjusts the normal pungency of the natural product, and flavors or spices can add profundity and intricacy to the taste.

Flexibility: a flexible fixing can be utilized in different ways. You can spread it on sandwiches, use it as a coating for broiled meats, blend it into sauces, or match it with cheddar and wafers.

Hand-crafted Enjoyment: Many individuals make tomato jam at home utilizing new, ready tomatoes. This takes into account the customization of fixings and flavors to suit individual inclinations.

Fixings: Normal fixings in tomato predicament incorporate tomatoes, sugar, vinegar (generally apple juice vinegar), and flavors like cinnamon, cloves, and ginger. A few recipes may likewise incorporate onions or red pepper for added intricacy.

Long Period of usability: Tomato jam can be canned and put away for a lengthy period, making it an incredible method for saving the kinds of ready summer tomatoes for use consistently.

Territorial Varieties: Various areas might have their varieties of tomato jam, with special fixings and flavor profiles because of neighborhood culinary practices.

Pairings: Tomato jam coordinates well with different food varieties, including cheddar, barbecued meats, burgers, and sandwiches. It can likewise be utilized as a plunge or fixing for tidbits.

Sweet and Appetizing Dishes: It's not only for exquisite applications; tomato jam can likewise be utilized in sweet dishes, like cakes and treats, where its sweet-tart flavor can add profundity.

Medical advantages: Tomatoes are a decent wellspring of nutrients and cell reinforcements, so tomato jam, when consumed with some restraint, can offer some medical advantages.

Culinary Innovativeness: Gourmet specialists and home cooks frequently use tomato jam to add a one-of-a-kind turn to recipes and investigations with various flavor blends.

In general, tomato jam is a wonderful and flexible sauce that can hoist the kinds of different dishes and give a sweet-flavorful kick to your culinary manifestations.

Absolutely! Here is an essential recipe for making hand-crafted tomato jam:

Fixings:

2 pounds (around 4 cups) ready tomatoes, finely hacked

2 cups granulated sugar

1/2 cup apple juice vinegar

1 little onion, finely hacked

1 clove garlic, minced

1 teaspoon salt

1/2 teaspoon ground cumin

1/2 teaspoon red pepper pieces (adapt to wanted hotness)

1/4 teaspoon ground cloves

1/4 teaspoon ground cinnamon

Directions:

Begin by whitening and stripping the tomatoes. Score the bottoms of the tomatoes with a shallow "X" and spot them in bubbling water for around 30 seconds. Then, move them to an ice water shower and the skins ought to handily strip off. Hack the striped tomatoes finely.

In a huge, weighty lined pot, consolidate the cleaved tomatoes, sugar, apple juice vinegar, hacked onion, minced garlic, and every one of the flavors. Mix to consolidate.

Heat the blend to the point of boiling over medium-high intensity, mixing habitually. When it arrives at a bubble, diminish the intensity to low and allow it to stew.

Keep stewing, and blending incidentally to forestall staying, until the combination thickens and arrives at a jam-like consistency. This can take somewhere in the range of 1 to 90 minutes, contingent upon the intensity and the water content of your tomatoes.

Taste the jam and change the flavoring if necessary, adding more sugar for pleasantness or more red pepper pieces for heat.

When the jam has thickened however you would prefer, eliminate it from the intensity and let it cool marginally.

Empty the hot tomato jam into cleaned containers and seal them. You can handle the containers in a hot water shower for a longer time frame of realistic usability or store them in the cooler for guaranteed use.

Recollect that natively constructed tomato jam considers adaptability as far as the flavors and flavorings you can utilize, so go ahead and tweak it as you would prefer. Partake in your custom-made tomato jam on sandwiches, with cheddar, or as a fix for different dishes!

Zucchini Relish

Zucchini relish is a sauce or side dish produced using zucchini, a sort of summer squash. It's regularly ready by hacking zucchini and consolidating it with different fixings like onions, vinegar, sugar, and different flavors. The combination is then cooked down to make a relish with a sweet and tart flavor. Zucchini relish can be utilized as a garnish for sausages, burgers, or sandwiches, or as a side dish to supplement various dishes. It's an incredible method for protecting zucchini and partake in its flavors all year.

Absolutely! Zucchini relish is a flexible topping that offers an interesting turn on customary relishes. Here are a few extra subtleties:

Fixings: Other than zucchini, normal fixings in zucchini relish might incorporate onions, ringer peppers, sugar, vinegar (generally white or juice vinegar), mustard seeds, celery seeds, and turmeric. These fixings give the relish its particular sweet and tart flavor.

Surface: Zucchini relish commonly has a thick surface, with little bits of zucchini and different vegetables blended in a tasty sugary fluid.

Utilizes: Zucchini relish is a scrumptious backup to different dishes. It may very well be served close to barbecued meats, added to sandwiches or wraps, or utilized as a garnish for franks, wieners, or burgers. It can likewise be integrated into recipes to add an eruption of flavor.

Protection: Zucchini relish is an incredible method for safeguarding a wealth of zucchini throughout the late spring months. Canning is a typical strategy to expand its time frame of realistic usability so you can appreciate it consistently.

Varieties: There are numerous varieties of zucchini relish, and recipes can shift by locale or individual inclination. Certain individuals add fixings like hot peppers for a zesty kick, while others might change the degree of pleasantness or corrosiveness to suit their taste.

In synopsis, zucchini relish is a delicious and flexible fix that utilizes zucchini and various fixings to make a sweet and tart backup for a large number of dishes.

Positively! Here is an essential recipe for natively constructed zucchini relish:

Fixings:

4 cups ground zucchini (around 4 medium-sized zucchinis)

2 cups finely slashed onions

1 red ringer pepper, finely hacked

1 green ringer pepper, finely hacked

1/4 cup salt

2 1/2 cups white or juice vinegar

2 1/2 cups granulated sugar

1 tablespoon mustard seeds

1/2 teaspoon celery seeds

1/2 teaspoon ground turmeric

Guidelines:

In an enormous blending bowl, consolidate the ground zucchini, slashed onions, and hacked ringer peppers. Sprinkle the salt over the vegetables and mix to join. Cover the combination with cold water and let it last 2 hours. Following 2 hours, channel the vegetables and flush them completely with cold water to eliminate overabundance of salt. Channel once more.

In an enormous, non-receptive pot, join the vinegar, sugar, mustard seeds, celery seeds, and ground turmeric. Heat the combination to the point of boiling, then, at that point, lessen the intensity and let it stew for 10 minutes.

Add the depleted and flushed zucchini, onions, and ringer peppers to the vinegar combination. Stew the combination for around 10-15 minutes, blending periodically, until the vegetables become delicate and the relish thickens.

While the relish is stewing, set up your canning containers and covers by sanitizing them in bubbling water.

When the relish has thickened however you would prefer, eliminate it from the intensity.

Cautiously spoon the hot zucchini relish into the cleaned canning containers, leaving around 1/4 inch of headspace at the highest point of each container.

Wipe the container edges clean and put the sanitized tops and rings on the containers, guaranteeing they're fixed but not excessively close.

Process the containers in a bubbling water shower for around 10-15 minutes to guarantee legitimate fixing.

Eliminate the containers from the water shower and let them cool. You ought to hear the covers pop as they seal.

When the containers have cooled, check to guarantee they are fixed appropriately. Any unlocked containers ought to be refrigerated and utilized within half a month.

Your natively constructed zucchini relish is currently prepared to appreciate or store in a cool, dull spot. It should keep going for as long as a year when appropriately fixed and put away.

Carrot and Ginger Chutney

Carrot and Ginger Chutney is a fix or sauce normally made by mixing or cooking together carrots, ginger, and different flavors. It can have a sweet and tart flavor with a sprinkle of zestiness from the ginger. This chutney is flexible and can be utilized as a plunge, spread, or backup to different dishes, like barbecued meats, sandwiches, or Indian food. The particular recipe can differ, yet it frequently incorporates fixings like carrots, ginger, vinegar, sugar, and flavors.

Positively! Carrot and Ginger Chutney is a wonderful and delightful fix that joins the normal pleasantness of carrots with the punch of new ginger. Here is an essential recipe:

Fixings:

2 cups ground carrots

2 tablespoons ground new ginger

1 cup sugar

1 cup vinegar (white or apple juice)

1 teaspoon red bean stew chips (conform to your favored degree of heat)

1 teaspoon salt

A touch of ground cinnamon (discretionary)

Directions:

In a pot, join the ground carrots, ginger, sugar, vinegar, bean stew pieces, and salt.

Cook over medium intensity, blending infrequently, until the combination thickens and the carrots become delicate, which can require around 20-30 minutes.

Whenever wanted, add a spot of ground cinnamon for additional character.

Allow the chutney to cool and afterward move it to a spotless, hermetically sealed holder. It will keep on thickening as it cools.

Store the Carrot and Ginger Chutney in the cooler. It tends to be delighted in as a fixation with different dishes or tidbits.

Go ahead and change the pleasantness, zestiness, and thickness to suit your taste. This chutney can be modified in numerous ways, and you can try different things with various flavors and flavors to make your exceptional variety.

Here is a straightforward recipe for Carrot and Ginger Chutney:

Fixings:

2 cups ground carrots

2 tablespoons ground new ginger

1 cup sugar

1 cup vinegar (white or apple juice)

1 teaspoon red bean stew chips (conform to your favored degree of heat)

1 teaspoon salt

A touch of ground cinnamon (discretionary)

Directions:

In a pot, join the ground carrots, ginger, sugar, vinegar, bean stew pieces, and salt.

Cook over medium intensity, blending infrequently, until the combination thickens and the carrots become delicate, which can require around 20-30 minutes.

Whenever wanted, add a spot of ground cinnamon for additional character.

Allow the chutney to cool and afterward move it to a spotless, impenetrable compartment. It will keep on thickening as it cools.

Store the Carrot and Ginger Chutney in the cooler. It tends to be delighted as a fixation with different dishes or bites.

Go ahead and change the pleasantness, hotness, and thickness to suit your taste. This chutney can be modified in numerous ways, and you can try different things with various flavors and flavors to make your one-of-a-kind variety. Appreciate!

Blueberry Preserves

Blueberry jam is a sort of natural product spread produced using blueberries. They are like jam or jam yet commonly contain bigger parts of natural products. Blueberries are cooked with sugar and here and there gelatin to make a sweet, thick, and stout spread that can be utilized as a garnish for different food varieties, like toast, hotcakes, or pastries.

Blueberry jams are normally made by stewing new or frozen blueberries with sugar and frequently gelatin, a characteristic gelling specialist tracked down in natural products. The sugar assists with saving the products of the soil's pleasantness, while gelatin thickens the combination into a spreadable consistency. The cooking system separates the blueberries and merges their flavors, bringing about a rich, sweet, and fruity spread with little bits of blueberry all through. Blueberry jam can be utilized in different culinary applications, from spreading on bread to filling baked goods or filling in as a sauce for meats and cheeses. They are a famous method for partaking in the kind of blueberries all year.

Here is a basic recipe for making custom-made blueberry jelly:

Fixings:

4 cups new or frozen blueberries

2 cups granulated sugar

1 tablespoon lemon juice (discretionary)

1 parcel (1.75 oz) natural product gelatin (discretionary, for added thickness)

Guidelines:

Wash the blueberries and eliminate any stems or leaves.

In an enormous pan, join the blueberries and sugar. If you favor a marginally tart flavor, you can add the lemon juice at this stage.

If you need a thicker consistency, you can blend in the organic product gelatin too. Adhere to the directions on the gelatin bundle for best outcomes.

Place the pot over medium intensity and mix the combination until the sugar has broken up.

When the sugar has broken up, heat the blend to the point of boiling. Decrease the intensity to a stew and let it cook for around 15-20 minutes, blending at times. The blend ought to thicken as it cooks.

To check the consistency, you can play out a "wrinkle test." Spot a limited quantity of the combination on a chilled plate and let it cool briefly. Then, at that point, push the blend with your finger, and assuming it wrinkles, it's prepared. If not, keep on stewing for a couple of additional minutes and test once more.

When the jam has arrived at the ideal thickness, eliminate the pan from the intensity and let it cool somewhat.

Empty the hot blueberry jelly into cleaned glass containers, leaving a little space at the top for extension. Seal the containers firmly.

Permit the containers to cool at room temperature, and you'll hear a fantastic "pop" as they seal. When they're cool, store them in the fridge for guaranteed use or cycle them for long-haul stockpiling.

These hand-crafted blueberry jams are perfect for spreading on toast, or biscuits, or involved in different recipes like cakes, yogurt parfaits, or as a frosting for meats. Appreciate!

Fruit and Vegetable Compotes

Products of the soil compotes are sweet, sugary dishes made by stewing lumps of foods grown from the ground/vegetables in a sugar or organic product juice combination until they become delicate and discharge their flavors. Compotes are frequently seasoned with flavors like cinnamon or vanilla. They can be filled in as a garnish for treats, a side dish, or even as a topping for different dishes. Compotes are a flexible method for partaking in the regular pleasantness of products of the soil.

Here are a few extra insights concerning leafy foods compotes:

Flexibility: Compotes can be made with a wide assortment of products of the soil, including apples, pears, berries, peaches, and rhubarb, and that's only the tip of the iceberg. They can likewise incorporate a blend of various foods grown from the ground for added intricacy.

Improving: Sugar is normally used to improve compotes, however, you can likewise utilize honey, maple syrup, or different sugars to taste. How much sugar is utilized can be changed given individual inclinations.

Cooking Cycle: Compotes are regularly cooked over low to medium intensity, permitting the natural product or vegetables to separate and deliver their juices. The blend is stewed until it thickens and takes on a sweet consistency.

Utilizes: Compotes are flexible and can be utilized in different ways. They can be served warm or chilled as a sweet all alone, as a garnish for frozen yogurt, yogurt, flapjacks, or waffles. They can likewise be utilized as a filling for pies, and cakes, or as a side dish for meats and poultry.

Safeguarding: Compotes can be canned or bumped to broaden their period of usability. Appropriately canned compotes can be put away for a considerable length of time.

Better Choice: Contrasted with numerous different treats, leafy foods compotes are a somewhat solid decision as they hold the regular flavors and supplements of the fixings, with negligible added sugar whenever wanted.

Occasional Fixings: Creating compotes with occasional foods grown from the ground can improve the flavors and newness of the dish.

In general, compotes are a magnificent method for partaking in the regular decency of products of the soil in a sweet and tasty structure.

Here is a straightforward recipe for an exemplary natural product compote:

Exemplary Natural product Compote

Fixings:

4 cups of blended natural products (e.g., apples, pears, berries, or any products of your decision)

1/2 cup granulated sugar (conform to taste)

1/2 cup water

1 teaspoon vanilla concentrate (discretionary)

1 cinnamon stick (discretionary)

Lemon juice (from a portion of a lemon)

Directions:

Strip and cleave the organic products into reduced-down pieces. Assuming that you're utilizing berries, you can leave them entirely.

In a pot, consolidate the hacked organic products, sugar, water, and cinnamon sticks (if utilized). Press the lemon juice over the natural products to add a sprinkle of sharpness.

Cook over medium intensity, mixing at times, until the sugar has broken up and the natural products start to deliver their juices. This ought to require around 5-10 minutes.

Lessen the intensity to low and stew the combination for 15-20 minutes, or until the natural products are delicate and the compote has thickened as you would prefer. You can crush the natural products somewhat with a fork for a chunkier surface or leave them as they are for a smoother compote.

In the case of utilizing vanilla concentrate, mix it into the compote toward the end.

Eliminate the cinnamon stick, and permit the compote to cool. You can serve it warm or chilled, contingent upon your inclination.

Partake in the natural product all alone, as a fix for frozen yogurt, yogurt, hotcakes, or some other sweet of your decision.

Go ahead and alter the products of the soil to suit your taste. You can likewise try different things with flavors like nutmeg or cloves for various varieties. Partake in your custom-made organic product compote!

Marmalade and Fruit butter

Surely! Here are recipes for both preserves and natural product margarine:

Orange Jelly:

Fixings:

4 huge oranges

1 lemon

4 cups of water

4 cups of sugar

Guidelines:

Wash the oranges and lemon completely. Slice them down the middle, and squeeze them. Save the seeds and tie them in a cheesecloth.

Cut the orange and lemon strips into dainty strips.

In a huge pot, consolidate the organic product juice, cut strips, water, and the cheesecloth pack of seeds. Stew for around 2 hours until the strips are delicate.

Eliminate the seed sack and dispose of it.

Add sugar to the pot and mix until it breaks up.

Keep on cooking over medium intensity, blending incidentally, until the combination thickens and arrives at the ideal consistency. This can require around 20-30 minutes.

Test for thickness just barely on a virus plate. If it sets, it's prepared.

Empty the preserves into cleaned containers and seal them.

Creamy fruit spread:

Fixings:

4 pounds of apples (stripped, cored, and cut)

1 cup of sugar

1 teaspoon of cinnamon

1/2 teaspoon of nutmeg

1/4 teaspoon of cloves

1/4 teaspoon of salt

Guidelines:

Place the cut apples in a sluggish cooker or enormous pot.

In a different bowl, blend the sugar, cinnamon, nutmeg, cloves, and salt.

Sprinkle the sugar-zest blend over the apples and mix to cover.

Cook the apples on low intensity for around 10-12 hours in a sluggish cooker or stew in a pot in the oven until the apples transform into a thick, dim-colored spread-like consistency.

Utilize a submersion blender to puree the combination until smooth. If you favor a chunkier surface, you can skirt this step.

Taste and change the pleasantness and flavor level as desired.

Spoon the creamy fruit spread into disinfected containers and seal.

Make sure to disinfect your containers and covers before filling them to guarantee the protection of your preserves and natural product spread. Partake in your hand-crafted treats!

Chapter 5: Freezing Vegetables

Blanching Techniques

Whitening is a cooking method that includes momentarily drenching food, regularly vegetables or natural products, in bubbling water, trailed by rapidly cooling them in ice water. The main roles of whitening are to:

Protect variety and flavor: Whitening assists with keeping up with the energetic variety and new kinds of food by deactivating proteins that can cause staining and loss of flavor.

Relax or to some extent cook: It can somewhat prepare the food, making it delicate while holding a fresh surface. This is valuable when you intend to freeze or store the nourishment for a lengthy period.

Eliminate debasements: Whitening can assist with eliminating surface soil, microorganisms, or solid flavors from specific food varieties.

The whitening system commonly includes the accompanying advances:

Heat a pot of water to the point of boiling.

Lower the food in the bubbling water for a brief period, typically one little while.

Immediately move the food to a bowl of ice water to stop the cooking system and protect its tone and surface.

Channel the food before involving it in your recipe.

Whitening is usually utilized for vegetables like broccoli, green beans, and carrots before freezing them. It's additionally utilized in certain recipes, such as whitened almonds for almond milk or whitened tomatoes for stripping the skin without any problem.

The following are a couple of additional insights regarding whitening:

Whitening Times: The whitening time can fluctuate contingent on the sort and size of the food. For instance, mixed greens could require a couple of moments, while thicker vegetables like carrots might require a little while. It's significant not to over-whiten, as this can bring about overcooking.

Ice Water Shower: The ice water shower is an essential move toward whitening. It quickly cools the food and stops the cooking system. It's prescribed to utilize ice water or freezing water with ice-solid shapes to guarantee a speedy cool-down.

Whitening Hardware: You can utilize a whitening container or an opened spoon to drench the food in bubbling water and eliminate it rapidly. Having a huge pot with a tight-fitting cover is likewise fundamental.

Stripping and Cleaning: Whitening is frequently utilized for natural products like tomatoes and peaches to make stripping the skin simpler. After whitening, the skin can be effortlessly taken out the hard way.

Whitening for Freezing: Many individuals whiten vegetables before freezing them. This helps protect their quality for longer periods in the cooler. In the wake of whitening, the food is typically dried and afterward bundled for freezing.

Wellbeing Note: Consistently work-out alert while working with bubbling water. Use utensils or an opened spoon to deal with the food and be aware of steam and sprinkles.

By and large, whitening is a flexible procedure utilized in different cooking situations to keep up with the newness and nature of food sources, particularly when conservation is a worry.

Here is a straightforward recipe for an exemplary dish: Spaghetti Carbonara.

Fixings:

12 ounces (340g) spaghetti

2 enormous eggs

1 cup (around 100g) ground Pecorino Romano cheddar (or Parmesan)

4-6 cuts of pancetta or guanciale (Italian relieved pork), diced

2 cloves garlic, minced (discretionary)

Salt and dark pepper to taste

New parsley, cleaved, for decorating (discretionary)

Directions:

Cook the spaghetti in a huge pot of salted bubbling water as per the bundle guidelines until still somewhat firm. Save around 1 cup of pasta cooking water, then, at that point, channel the pasta.

While the pasta is cooking, in a bowl, whisk together the eggs, ground cheddar, and a liberal measure of dark pepper. Put this blend away.

In a huge skillet, cook the diced pancetta or guanciale over medium intensity until it becomes fresh and brilliant brown. In the case of utilizing garlic, add it to the container and sauté for about a moment until fragrant. Eliminate the dish from heat.

Following depleting the cooked pasta, add it to the skillet with the firm pancetta. Throw to consolidate and cover the pasta with the delivered fat.

Immediately pour the egg and cheddar blend over the hot pasta. Throw everything together enthusiastically, utilizing a touch of the held pasta cooking water if necessary to make a velvety sauce. The intensity of the pasta will cook the eggs and make a rich, messy sauce.

Taste and change the flavoring with salt and pepper if vital.

Serve the spaghetti carbonara right away, decorated with more ground cheddar, dark pepper, and hacked new parsley whenever you want.

Partake in your natively constructed Spaghetti Carbonara! It's an exemplary Italian pasta dish that is rich, velvety, and brimming with flavor.

Freezer Bag and Tray Methods

Cooler pack and plate strategies are two normal procedures for freezing food to safeguard it for longer periods.

Cooler Sack Strategy: In this technique, you place the food thing, like natural products, vegetables, or meat, in a cooler-safe plastic pack. Eliminate however much air as could reasonably be expected from the sack to forestall cooler consumption. Seal the sack firmly and mark it with the items and date. Then, at that point, you can lay the packs level in the cooler, which considers simple stacking and effective utilization of cooler space.

Plate Strategy: This technique is frequently utilized for freezing things that are in a fluid or semi-fluid state, similar to soups, sauces, or purees. You empty the fluid into an ice 3D square plate, biscuit tin, or comparable compartment. Whenever it's frozen, you can jump out the singular parcels and move them to a cooler sack. This strategy is perfect for segment control and speedy admittance to little servings of food.

The two techniques help to forestall cooler consumption and keep up with the nature of your food. The decision between these techniques relies upon the kind of food you're freezing and your stockpiling inclinations.

Here are a few extra insights regarding the cooler pack and plate strategies:

Cooler Sack Technique (proceeded):

While utilizing the cooler sack technique, it's fundamental to pick cooler-safe packs, which are intended to endure low temperatures and keep the packs from becoming weak or tearing in the cooler.

Crush out however much air as could reasonably be expected before fixing the pack to limit the gamble of cooler consumption. Certain individuals utilize a straw to assist with eliminating the overabundance of air from the sack.

Marking the packs with the items and date is critical for simple ID later, assisting you with keeping away from disarray about what's put away in the sacks.

This technique is flexible and can be utilized for many food varieties, from products of the soil to meats and arranged feasts.

Plate Technique (proceeded):

The plate technique is especially valuable for food varieties that you need to freeze in little, individual bits. For instance, you can freeze custom-made child food, stock, or spices thusly.

When the food is frozen on the plate, you can move the bits to a marked cooler pack or impermeable compartment. This makes it simple to get the ideal amount when you want it without thawing out the whole bunch.

Utilizing a silicone ice shape plate can be advantageous for this strategy, as the segments are not difficult to jump out once frozen.

This technique functions admirably for fluids and semi-fluids yet may not be appropriate for bigger, strong food things.

In the two techniques, it's vital to store food at a reliable, low temperature to keep up with its quality and forestall waste. Moreover, legitimate bundling and naming are critical to guaranteeing that your frozen food stays coordinated and holds its flavor and surface when you in the end use it.

I can give you a recipe! Kindly determine the sort of recipe you're keen on or on the other hand if you have specific inclinations, like a particular cooking or dietary limitations. This will assist me with giving you a more customized recipe.

Indeed, here are a few different recipes for you:

Exemplary Spaghetti Carbonara:

Fixings:

12 ounces (340g) spaghetti

2 huge eggs

1 cup ground Pecorino Romano cheddar

4 ounces (113g) pancetta or guanciale, diced

2 cloves garlic, minced

Newly ground dark pepper

New parsley, hacked (for decorating)

Directions:

Cook the spaghetti as per bundle guidelines until still somewhat firm.

In a different bowl, whisk together the eggs and ground cheddar. Season with dark pepper.

In a skillet, cook the pancetta or guanciale until firm. Add the minced garlic and sauté momentarily.

Channel the cooked spaghetti, and keeping in mind that it's as yet hot, immediately throw it with the egg and cheddar blend until the pasta is covered and rich.

Add the pancetta and garlic, and throw to consolidate.

Serve right away, embellished with cleaved new parsley.

Vegetable Pan fried food with Tofu:

Fixings:

1 block of extra-firm tofu, cubed

2 cups of blended vegetables (broccoli, ringer peppers, snap peas, carrots, and so forth.)

2 cloves garlic, minced

2 tablespoons soy sauce

1 tablespoon sesame oil

1 tablespoon vegetable oil

1 teaspoon ground new ginger

Cooked rice or noodles (for serving)

Guidelines:

Press the tofu to eliminate the overabundance of water by setting it between paper towels with a load on top for 15-30 minutes. Cut it into 3D shapes.

Heat the vegetable oil in a wok or huge skillet over medium-high intensity.

Add the tofu 3D shapes and pan-fried food until they're brilliant and fresh. Eliminate from the skillet and put away.

In a similar dish, add a smidgen more oil if necessary. Pan-sear the blended vegetables, garlic, and ginger until they're delicate yet fresh.

Return the tofu to the container, and add soy sauce and sesame oil. Throw all that to join.

Serve the pan-fried food over prepared rice or noodles.

Partake in these delightful recipes!

Proper Storage

Appropriate vegetable stockpiling is essential to keep up with newness and broaden the period of usability of your produce. Here are a few general tips:

Refrigeration: Most vegetables ought to be put away in the cooler. Utilize the vegetable crisper cabinet, which has customizable stickiness settings.

Temperature: Keep the cooler at the right temperature, commonly around 35-40°F (1-4°C).

Dampness: Vegetables have different dampness necessities. Utilize higher mugginess settings for salad greens and lower dampness for things like peppers and cucumbers.

Ethylene Gas: A few natural products discharge ethylene gas, which can speed up the maturing and deterioration of vegetables. Store ethylene-delivering organic products like apples, bananas, and avocados independently.

Ventilation: Guarantee great air dissemination in the cooler to forestall the development of dampness.

Capacity Compartments: Utilize punctured plastic sacks or vegetable-explicit capacity holders to assist with keeping up with the right degree of mugginess.

Root Vegetables: Store root vegetables like carrots and potatoes in a cool, dull spot, away from onions, which can influence their flavor.

Spices: Store spices with stems in a glass of water, covering them with a plastic pack.

Tomatoes: Keep tomatoes at room temperature until they age, then move them to the cooler to broaden their time of usability.

Mixed Greens: Eliminate any groups, ties, or elastic groups from greens to keep them from getting excessively close and shrinking.

Recollect that these are basic rules, and a few vegetables have explicit capacity needs. Continuously check for individual proposals for each kind of produce, and attempt to utilize them inside their prescribed periods to partake in the best flavor and sustenance.

Using Frozen Vegetables in Recipes

Frozen vegetables can be a helpful and nutritious expansion to numerous recipes. Simply follow these tips:

Defrosting: A few recipes might expect you to defrost the frozen vegetables first. You can do this by leaving them in the fridge for a couple of hours or involving the thaw-out capability in your microwave.

Cooking: Cook the frozen vegetables as indicated by the recipe guidelines, whether it's bubbling, steaming, simmering, or sautéing. Remember that frozen vegetables might require a piece longer cooking time than new ones.

Preparing: Season the frozen vegetables with spices, flavors, and flavors to improve their flavor. Garlic, olive oil, and lemon juice function admirably with many frozen veggies.

Surface: Focus on the ideal surface in your recipe. A few vegetables, similar to peas or corn, can be added straightforwardly to a dish, while others might profit from whitening or fractional cooking before consolidating them.

Blend and Match: Trial with various frozen vegetable mixes in your recipes to change it up and nourish.

Healthy benefit: Frozen vegetables are ordinarily picked at their pinnacle readiness and frozen, saving their supplements. They can be a solid expansion to your dinners.

Capacity: Store any unused frozen vegetables appropriately in a fixed holder or cooler sack to forestall cooler consumption.

Positively! Here are a few explicit thoughts for involving frozen vegetables in different recipes:

Pan sear: Frozen blended vegetables, similar to sauté mixes, function admirably in pan sear dishes. Simply throw them into the skillet with your decision of protein and pan-fried food sauce for a speedy and simple feast.

Soup: Add frozen vegetables to soups and stews for added nourishment and flavor. They can be a helpful method for supporting the vegetable substance of your natively constructed soup.

Meals: Integrate frozen vegetables into goulashes, like lasagna, shepherd's pie, or prepared pasta dishes. Blend them in with different elements for a total feast.

Seared Rice: Frozen peas and carrots are extraordinary augmentations to natively constructed broiled rice. They cook rapidly and add tone and surface to the dish.

Omelets and Quiches: Sprinkle a small bunch of frozen spinach or blended vegetables into your morning omelet or a flavorful quiche for a sound breakfast or early lunch.

Side Dishes: Steam or sauté frozen vegetables like broccoli, green beans, or Brussels sprouts as a side dish, and season with your number one spices and flavors.

Smoothies: While not a common cooking technique, you can likewise add frozen spinach or kale to your morning meal smoothies for a nutritious lift. Whether you're making sautés, soups, or meals, frozen vegetables can be an efficient and flexible fix in your cooking.

Recall that the particular cooking times and techniques might differ depending upon the kind of frozen vegetables and your recipe, so make certain to adhere to the recipe directions for the best outcomes. Utilizing frozen vegetables can save you time and diminish food squandering while also giving a nutritious part to your dinners.

Freeze-Drying Vegetables

Freeze-drying, otherwise called lyophilization, is a food conservation strategy that includes freezing an item and afterward eliminating the ice by sublimation, which is the progress of a substance straightforwardly from a string to a gas without going through the fluid stage. On account of vegetables, freeze-drying includes freezing them, decreasing the encompassing tension, and afterward leisurely warming them. This interaction eliminates dampness from the vegetables, safeguarding their surface, flavor, and dietary substance while expanding their time of usability. The subsequent freeze-dried vegetables are lightweight, have a long time frame of realistic usability, and can be rehydrated by adding water, making them a helpful choice for setting up camp, crisis food supplies, and space travel.

Freeze-drying vegetables includes a few stages:

Freezing: Vegetables are first stuck to an exceptionally low temperature. This freezing step assists with securing the newness and supplements of the vegetables.

Vacuum Chamber: The frozen vegetables are put in a vacuum chamber. In this chamber, the gaseous tension is decreased, which permits the frozen water in the vegetables to sublimate straightforwardly from ice to fume without going through the fluid stage.

Drying: As the tension abates in the vacuum chamber, the temperature is gradually raised. This cycle empowers the frozen water in the vegetables to transform from a string to a gas, successfully eliminating the dampness from the vegetables.

Bundling: When the freeze-drying process is finished, the dried vegetables are ordinarily fixed in water/airproof holders to keep dampness and oxygen from returning. This bundling assists with keeping up with the vegetables' long period of usability.

The subsequent freeze-dried vegetables hold their unique shape, variety, flavor, and a large portion of their dietary benefit, which goes with them a famous decision for protecting vegetables for long haul stockpiling or for use in items like moment soups, exploring dinners, and space traveler food. At the point when you need to utilize freeze-dried vegetables, you can rehydrate them by adding water, and they will recover quite a bit of their unique surface and taste.

Positively! Here is a straightforward recipe for rehydrating and involving freeze-dried vegetables in a vegetable pan-fried food:

Fixings:

1 cup of freeze-dried blended vegetables (e.g., peas, carrots, ringer peppers)

1 tablespoon vegetable oil

1 clove of garlic, minced

1/2 onion, cut

1 cup of cooked rice or noodles

2 tablespoons soy sauce

Salt and pepper to taste

Discretionary: your decision of protein (tofu, chicken, shrimp, and so forth.)

Guidelines:

Rehydrate the Vegetables:

Place the freeze-dried vegetables in a bowl.

Pour bubbling water over them to cover and allow them to sit for around 5-7 minutes until they have rehydrated and become delicate.

Channel any overabundance of water.

Set up Your Protein (if utilizing):

If you're adding protein, cook it in a different skillet with a touch of oil until it's cooked through. Put it away.

Pan sear:

Heat the vegetable oil in an enormous skillet or wok over medium-high intensity.

Add the minced garlic and cut onion. Sauté for several minutes until they become fragrant and the onion turns clear.

Add the Dehydrated Vegetables:

Add the rehydrated freeze-dried vegetables to the skillet. Pan sear for a couple of moments until they are warmed through.

Add Cooked Rice or Noodles:

Add the cooked rice or noodles to the skillet and mix it with the vegetables.

Season:

Pour the soy sauce over the sautéed food and blend well. Season with salt and pepper to taste. Change the flavoring to your inclination.

Protein:

Assuming that you arranged protein in sync 2, add it to the sautéed food as of now and blend it in.

Serve:

Whenever everything is warmed through and all around consolidated, serve your vegetable pan-fried food hot. You can embellish it with sesame seeds or cleaved green onions for additional flavor and show.

This recipe is flexible, and you can redo it with your number one vegetables and protein decisions. Freeze-dried vegetables make it simple to mix up veggies in your pan-fried food, and they rehydrate rapidly for a helpful feast.

Chapter 6: Drying Vegetables

Sun Drying

Sun drying is a technique for safeguarding food by presenting it to the sun's intensity and normal light, commonly in an open region. This interaction eliminates dampness from the food, which represses the development of microorganisms and forestall waste. Sun drying is regularly utilized for natural products, vegetables, spices, and specific kinds of meat or fish. It's an old and customary food protection procedure, yet current strategies like dehydrators are additionally utilized for a similar reason.

Surely! Sun drying includes a few stages:

Readiness: Food things are cleaned, cut, or cleaved into the ideal size and thickness to work with drying. This assists in uncovering a bigger surface region to the sun and paces up the drying with handling.

Drying surface: Food is regularly spread out on perfect, level surfaces like plates, racks, or mats. These surfaces ought to take into consideration great air dissemination to guarantee in any event, drying.

Sun openness: The pre-arranged food is put in direct daylight, in a perfect world on a radiant and dry day. The sun's intensity and energy make the dampness inside the food vanish continuously.

Turning and covering: During the drying system, the food might be gone occasionally to guarantee uniform drying. It might likewise be covered with a spotless material or work to shield it from residue, bugs, or birds.

Length: The time expected for sun drying fluctuates depending on factors like food type, thickness, weather patterns, and the strength of the sun. It can require a few days to weeks to finish the cycle.

Testing for doneness: To decide whether the food is satisfactorily dried, you can play out a straightforward test. Natural products, for instance, ought to be flexible, not tacky, and spices ought to disintegrate effectively when squashed.

Sun drying is a financially savvy and energy-productive strategy for food protection, however, it's profoundly reliant upon the environment and weather patterns. In locales with reliable daylight and low dampness, it's a reasonable method for broadening the timeframe of realistic usability of different food varieties.

Without a doubt, here's a basic sun-dried tomato recipe:

Fixings:

Tomatoes (Roma or plum tomatoes function admirably)

Salt

Olive oil (discretionary)

Directions:

Wash and dry the tomatoes.

Cut the tomatoes in half the long way.

Sprinkle some salt on the cut side of every tomato half.

Place the tomato parts, cut side up, on a plate or a wire rack.

Forget about them in direct daylight for a few days. Try to cover them with a lattice or cheesecloth to shield them from bugs and flotsam and jetsam.

Bring them inside around evening time or on the other hand if there's an opportunity of downpour.

Contingent upon the climate and the thickness of the tomatoes, it might require 4-7 days for them to completely sun-dry. They ought to become rugged and somewhat contracted.

You can involve these sun-dried tomatoes in different recipes, similar to pasta dishes, mixed greens, or as a delightful expansion to sandwiches. You can likewise store them in impenetrable compartments with a touch of olive oil for added flavor and protection.

Surely, there's another sun-dried recipe, this time for making a sun-dried natural product:

Fixings:

Products of your decision (e.g., apricots, cherries, grapes, or plums)

Guidelines:

Wash and wipe off the organic products.

Cut bigger natural products fifty and eliminate pits or seeds if important.

To accelerate the drying system, you can whiten the organic products in bubbling water briefly and afterward drive them into ice water before sun-drying. This can assist with safeguarding the organic product's tone and flavor.

Put the pre-arranged natural products on plates or racks in a solitary layer.

Cover them with a fine cross-section or cheesecloth to shield them from bugs and trash.

Set the plate out in direct daylight for a few days. You might have to pivot the plate to guarantee in any event, drying.

Bring the plate inside around evening time or on the other hand if there's an opportunity of a downpour.

The drying time will rely upon the kind of natural product, weather patterns, and daylight, yet it can take anywhere from a couple of days to a long time.

Sun-dried natural products can be appreciated as bites, added to prepared merchandise, or utilized in servings of mixed greens and exquisite dishes. Try to store them in water/airproof holders once they're completely dried to keep them new.

Oven Drying

Stove drying is a technique for eliminating dampness from food or different substances by putting them in a broiler at a low temperature for a drawn-out period. It's usually utilized for protecting natural products, vegetables, spices, or in any event, making meat jerky. The low intensity dries out the material while holding its flavor and healthy benefits.

Broiler drying regularly includes putting the food or substance on baking sheets or racks in a solitary layer. The stove is set to a low temperature, for the most part between 140°F to 200°F (60°C to 93°C), and the entryway is in many cases left marginally unlatched to permit dampness to get away. The drying time can differ contingent upon the thing being dried, yet it can require a few hours to a day or more. The objective is to eliminate sufficient dampness to forestall decay while saving the taste and nature of the item.

Absolutely! The following are a couple of stove-drying recipes for different things:

Stove Dried Tomatoes:

Cut ready tomatoes into dainty rounds.

Put them on a baking sheet, shower with olive oil, and sprinkle with salt and spices (like basil or oregano).

Dry in a preheated stove at 175°F (80°C) for around 6-8 hours until they are dried yet at the same time marginally malleable.

Broiler Dried Spices:

Collect new spices (like basil, thyme, or rosemary).

Eliminate the leaves from the stems and spread them on a baking sheet.

Dry in a broiler set to its lowest temperature for 2-4 hours, or until the spices disintegrate without any problem.

Stove Dried Organic product Chips:

Cut natural products like apples, pears, or bananas into dainty cuts.

Orchestrate the cuts on a baking sheet, and you can sprinkle them with cinnamon or sugar whenever you want.

Dry in a preheated broiler at 140°F (60°C) for 3-4 hours until they're firm.

Broiler Dried Meat Jerky:

Cut the incline hamburger toward dainty strips.

Marinate the strips in your decision of preparing (e.g., soy sauce, Worcestershire sauce, and flavors).

Orchestrate the marinated strips on baking racks.

Dry on a stove at 160-180°F (71-82°C) for 4-6 hours, or until they are completely dried and jerky-like.

Stove Dried Mushrooms:

Cut or quarter new mushrooms.

Put them on a baking sheet, shower with olive oil, and sprinkle with salt and pepper.

Dry in a preheated stove at 150°F (65°C) for 2-3 hours, or until they're dried and marginally fresh.

Make sure to change drying times given the thickness and dampness content of the things you're drying. Furthermore, trying different things with various flavors and flavors can assist with making exceptional and scrumptious stove-dried tidbits and fixings.

Dehydrator Methods

Dehydrator strategies include eliminating dampness from food to safeguard it. There are a couple of normal strategies:

Electric Dehydrators: These machines use warming components and fans to circle warm air and eliminate dampness from food.

Sun-oriented Dehydrators: They utilize the sun's intensity to dry food. These are much of the time utilized in regions with adequate daylight.

Air Drying: This customary technique includes setting food in a very much-ventilated region to dry normally, for example, hanging spices or bean stew peppers.

Broiler Drying: You can utilize your stove at a low temperature to get dried-out food, yet it's less energy-productive than devoted dehydrators.

Microwave Drying: While not as normal, certain individuals use microwaves for limited-scope parchedness.

The decision of technique relies upon the sort of food you're drying and the gear you have accessible. Getting dried out is a helpful method for broadening the timeframe of realistic usability of organic products, vegetables, and spices, and that's only the tip of the iceberg.

Surely! Here's more data on dehydrator techniques:

Freeze Drying: This is a business strategy that eliminates dampness from food while it's frozen. It's known for saving the flavor and surface of the food astoundingly well.

Food Desiccants: These are little bundles or sachets that can be set with dried-out food to assimilate any excess dampness and assist with keeping the food dry during stockpiling.

Sun Drying: In regions with a ton of daylight and low mugginess, you can spread food out in the sun to normally get dried out. This technique is frequently utilized for things like raisins and sun-dried tomatoes.

Jerky and Meat Drying out: Making jerky includes marinating and afterward getting dried out meat to safeguard it. Many individuals utilize specific meat dehydrators or stoves for this reason.

Layering and Plate: Dehydrators frequently accompany numerous plates or layers to at the same time take into consideration the proficient drying of various food varieties.

Remember that various food sources might require explicit strategies and temperatures for getting dried out, so observing rules or recipes for the best results is significant. Got dried-out food varieties are perfect for bites, hiking, and long-haul stockpiling.

Absolutely! The following are a couple of dehydrator recipes for normal dried-out food sources:

Natural product Chips:

Cut natural products like apples, bananas, or strawberries into slim, uniform pieces.

Orchestrate them on a dehydrator plate.

Set the dehydrator to a temperature around 135°F (57°C) and let them dry for 8-12 hours or until they're firm.

Meat Jerky:

Cut incline meat toward dainty strips.

Marinate the strips in a combination of soy sauce, Worcestershire sauce, and your selection of flavors.

Organize the marinated strips on a dehydrator plate.

Dry them at a temperature of 160-165°F (71-74°C) for around 4-6 hours until they are dry yet at the same time adaptable.

Spice Drying:

Reap new spices like basil, oregano, or thyme.

Spread them in a solitary layer on a dehydrator plate.

Utilize the most minimal temperature setting, ordinarily around 95°F (35°C), and dry until the spices are weak, normally 2-4 hours.

Natural product Calfskin (Natural product Roll-Ups):

Puree-ready natural products like berries or mangoes.

Spread the puree on a dehydrator plate or material paper.

Get dried out at a low temperature of around 135°F (57°C) for 6-8 hours until the organic product cowhide is at this point not tacky.

Dried Vegetables:

Cut or cleave vegetables like carrots, ringer peppers, or zucchini.

Organize them on a dehydrator plate.

Dry at a temperature of 125-135°F (52-57°C) until they are totally dry, which can require 6-12 hours, contingent upon the vegetable.

These recipes give a decent beginning stage, however, you can change fixings and flavors to suit your taste. Make certain to keep the particular rules for your dehydrator model, as drying times and temperatures might fluctuate.

Rehydrating and Using Dried Vegetables

Rehydrating and utilizing dried vegetables is a helpful method for having nutritious fixings close by for cooking. Here is a general aide on the most proficient method to make it happen:

Choosing Dried Vegetables: Begin by picking great quality dried vegetables. They ought to be liberated from added substances and impurities. You can find dried vegetables in most supermarkets or on the web.

Rehydration: To rehydrate dried vegetables, place them in a bowl or pot, and cover them with heated water. The water ought to be hot, yet not bubbling. Allow them to drench for around 20-30 minutes, or until they become full and delicate.

Depleting: After rehydration, channel the abundance of water. You can save the fluid to use as vegetable stock in recipes whenever you want.

Utilizing Dehydrated Vegetables: Dehydrated vegetables can be utilized in different dishes, like soups, stews, galoshes, and sautés. They might have a marginally unexpected surface in comparison to new vegetables, so consider their cooking time in your recipes.

Flavor and Preparing: Dried vegetables can assimilate enhancement well, so season them as per your recipe. You might have to change the cooking time and flavors in light of the particular vegetable.

Capacity: Store any unused dehydrated vegetables in a sealed shut holder in the cooler. They ought to be utilized within a couple of days.

Remember that the rehydration time might differ depending on the kind and size of the dried vegetables. Continuously look at the bundle for particular guidelines, and change your cooking in a manner.

Surely, here's some more data about rehydrating and utilizing dried vegetables:

Benefits of Dried Vegetables:

The long time frame of realistic usability: Dried vegetables have a significantly longer period of usability contrasted with new ones, making them incredible for crisis food supplies and as a reinforcement for when new produce isn't free.

Accommodation: They are lightweight and don't need refrigeration, making them ideal for setting up camp, climbing, and other outside exercises.

Supplement Maintenance: Dried vegetables can hold a decent piece of their unique supplements, particularly when appropriately put away.

Tips for Rehydration:

Planning: Cut huge dried vegetables into more modest pieces before rehydrating to guarantee in any event, dowsing and cooking.

Mixing: Periodically mix the vegetables while rehydrating them to assist them with retaining water uniformly.

Heating up: A few vegetables might profit from a speedy bubble after rehydration to guarantee they are completely delicate and protected to eat.

Recipes Utilizing Dehydrated Vegetables:

Soups: Add dehydrated vegetables to soups like minestrone, vegetable, or bean soup.

Stews: They function admirably in generous stews and stew recipes.

Curries: Incorporate dehydrated vegetables in different curries for added surface and flavor.

Pasta Dishes: Blend them into pasta sauces or meals.

Sautés: Rehydrated vegetables can be utilized in pan-sears close by new fixings.

Mixed greens: Consolidate dehydrated vegetables into plates of mixed greens for added surface and sustenance.

Recollect that the rehydrated vegetables ought to be delicate and completely cooked before serving. The particular rehydration time will rely upon the vegetable, so analysis and taste as you go to accomplish the ideal surface.

Making Vegetable Chips and Jerky

Vegetable chips and jerky are made by getting dried out or baking vegetables. For vegetable chips, cuts of vegetables like potatoes, yams, or zucchini are frequently prepared and afterward heated until they become fresh. Jerky, then again, is made by meagerly cutting vegetables and marinating them in a tasty combination, then, at that point, getting dried out until they have a chewy surface like customary meat jerky. These tidbits are a better option in contrast to conventional potato chips and meat jerky.

Positively! Here is somewhat more detail on how vegetable chips and jerky are normally made:

Vegetable Chips:

Vegetable Determination: Pick a vegetable, similar to potatoes, yams, beets, or zucchini.

Cutting: The vegetables are cut daintily utilizing a mandoline slicer or a blade. More slender cuts will generally become crispier.

Preparing: The cuts are prepared with flavors, salt, and some of the time a modest quantity of oil to add flavor.

Baking/Getting dried out: The carefully prepared cuts are fanned out on baking sheets and heated in a broiler at a low temperature or dried out utilizing a food dehydrator. This interaction eliminates dampness, making them fresh.

Vegetable Jerky:

Vegetable Determination: Like chips, different vegetables can be utilized, with portobello mushrooms, eggplants, and carrots being well-known decisions.

Cutting: The vegetables are daintily cut or cut into strips.

Marinating: The cuts/strips are marinated in a combination of tasty fixings like soy sauce, flavors, fluid smoke, and sugars. This step bestows the jerky's trademark flavor.

Getting dried out: The marinated vegetable cuts are then dried out at a low temperature. This cycle eliminates dampness and concentrates the flavors, bringing about a chewy jerky-like surface.

The two techniques are better options in contrast to conventional nibble choices, as they are lower in fat and frequently higher in supplements because of the negligible handling included.

Here are fundamental recipes for making vegetable chips and jerky at home:

Vegetable Chips:

Fixings:

Vegetables of your decision (potatoes, yams, beets, zucchini, and so on.)

Olive oil (or oil of your decision)

Salt and pepper

Flavors of your choice (paprika, garlic powder, rosemary, and so on.)

Directions:

Preheat your stove to 375°F (190°C).

Wash and strip (if essential) the vegetables, and cut them into dainty, uniform rounds utilizing a mandoline slicer or a sharp blade.

In a bowl, throw the vegetable cuts with a touch of olive oil, salt, pepper, and your selection of flavors. Ensure they're equitably covered.

Organize the carefully prepared cuts on a baking sheet in a solitary layer, guaranteeing they don't cover.

Prepare in the preheated broiler for around 20-30 minutes, flipping the cuts part of the way through, until they are fresh and brilliant brown.

Eliminate them from the stove and let them cool before partaking in your natively constructed vegetable chips.

Vegetable Jerky:

Fixings:

Vegetables (e.g., portobello mushrooms, eggplants, carrots)

Soy sauce (or tamari for a without gluten choice)

Fluid smoke (for a smoky character)

Maple syrup (or your favored sugar)

Flavors of your choice (garlic powder, onion powder, paprika, and so on.)

Directions:

Cut your picked vegetables into slim strips.

In a bowl, join soy sauce, a couple of drops of fluid smoke, a shower of maple syrup, and your selection of flavors. Change the amounts to taste.

Add the vegetable strips to the marinade, ensuring they're uniformly covered. Permit them to marinate for no less than 30 minutes, or even for the time being for more extraordinary character.

Preheat your food dehydrator as indicated by the producer's guidelines.

Lay the marinated vegetable strips on the dehydrator plate, guaranteeing they have some space between them for legitimate air flow.

Get the strips dried out at a low temperature (as a rule around 125°F or 52°C) for 6-8 hours or until they arrive at the ideal jerky-like surface.

Allow them to cool and store your hand-crafted vegetable jerky in an impermeable holder.

Go ahead and redo these recipes with your number one flavors and flavor mixes to suit your inclinations.

Partake in your natively constructed vegetable chips and jerky!

Chapter 7: Fermentation Techniques

Lacto-Fermented Vegetables

Lacto-matured vegetables are a kind of saved food made by aging vegetables in a brackish water arrangement. This cycle depends on gainful microscopic organisms, like lactobacillus, to change over sugars into lactic corrosive, which goes about as a characteristic additive. It's an incredible method for making delectable and probiotic-rich food varieties like sauerkraut and kimchi. Here is an essential outline of the interaction for making lacto-matured vegetables:

Pick your vegetables: You can age various vegetables like cabbage, cucumbers, and carrots, and the sky's the limit from there. Wash and cleave them into your ideal shapes.

Set up a saline solution: Disintegrate salt in water to make a brackish water arrangement. The salt focus is commonly around 2-3% of the water weight, yet this can differ contingent on your taste.

Pack the vegetables: Spot the cleaved vegetables in a perfect, sealed shut holder or maturing vessel. Press them down to eliminate air holes.

Add flavorings: You can add flavors, spices, or garlic to improve the flavor.

Pour the salt water: Cover the vegetables with the saline solution, guaranteeing they're completely lowered. Utilize a weight or a cabbage leaf to keep them beneath the saline solution surface.

Aging time: Seal the holder and let it mature at room temperature, normally for 1 to about 14 days. Taste en route to screen the flavor.

Store: When the ideal flavor is accomplished, move the holder to the fridge to dial back the maturation cycle.

Lacto-matured vegetables are a solid and delicious expansion to your eating routine, because of the helpful microbes they contain. Try different things with various vegetables and flavors to make novel flavors!

Unquestionably! Here is a fundamental recipe for making lacto-matured vegetables, like sauerkraut. You can change the fixings and flavors to suit your taste inclinations:

Fixings:

1 medium head of cabbage

1-2 tablespoons of salt (non-iodized)

Discretionary flavorings: caraway seeds, garlic, juniper berries, and so forth.

Guidelines:

Eliminate the external leaves of the cabbage and put them away. These will be utilized later to cover the destroyed cabbage.

Shred the cabbage finely utilizing a blade or a food processor. You can likewise utilize a mandoline for uniform thickness.

Place the destroyed cabbage in a huge blending bowl. Sprinkle the salt over the cabbage.

Start to knead the cabbage and salt together. This will assist with delivering the cabbage's normal juices, making brackish water. Keep kneading for around 5-10 minutes.

Assuming you're adding discretionary flavorings, blend them into the cabbage.

Move the cabbage and any fluid it delivers into a spotless, disinfected glass or clay compartment. Press the cabbage down with a perfect, cleaned weight to guarantee it's completely lowered in its juices.

Place a couple of the external cabbage leaves you put away on top of the destroyed cabbage. This will assist with keeping the cabbage lowered.

Cover the compartment with a spotless fabric or a top that permits gas to escape, as gasses will be delivered during maturation.

Permit the holder to sit at room temperature (in a perfect world around 65-75°F or 18-24°C) for 1 to about fourteen days. Check it occasionally and press the cabbage down assuming that it transcends the fluid.

Taste the sauerkraut after about seven days, and assuming it has the ideal degree of maturation, move it to the cooler to dial back the aging system.

Your hand-crafted sauerkraut is presently prepared to appreciate! You can involve this essential technique as a layout and examination with various vegetables and flavors to make an assortment of lacto-matured vegetables.

Sauerkraut and Kimchi Fermentation

Sauerkraut and kimchi are both aged cabbage dishes. Maturation is a cycle where microorganisms, ordinarily lactic corrosive microscopic organisms, separate sugars in the cabbage, delivering lactic corrosive and giving these food sources their tart flavor. The key advances engaged with their maturation cycle include:

Setting up the Cabbage: Cabbage is destroyed or slashed and frequently blended in with salt to make brackish water. This salt assists with drawing out dampness from the cabbage.

Maturation Holder: The cabbage is pressed into a maturation compartment, for example, a glass container or clay vessel. It's crucial to pack it firmly to dispose of air and establish an anaerobic climate.

Lactic Corrosive Microbes: Normally happening lactic corrosive microorganisms or a starter culture might be added. These microbes convert the sugars in the cabbage into lactic corrosive, which jelly and flavors the food.

Maturation Time: The holder is left at room temperature for a while, normally a few days to weeks, permitting the cabbage to age. During this time, the flavor is created and the cabbage becomes harsh.

Capacity: When the ideal degree of maturation is accomplished, sauerkraut and kimchi can be put away in a cool spot, similar to a fridge, to dial back the aging system.

Sauerkraut is a German dish produced using matured white cabbage, frequently prepared with caraway seeds. Kimchi, then again, is a Korean dish produced using matured napa cabbage and frequently incorporates fixings like red pepper drops, garlic, ginger, and fish sauce, giving it a hot and sharp flavor. Both are famous for their special taste and the probiotics that result from the aging system, which can have potential medical advantages.

Here's more data about sauerkraut and kimchi maturation:

Sauerkraut:

Beginning: Sauerkraut is accepted to have begun in Germany and has been a customary food in numerous European nations.

Fixings: The primary fixing is white cabbage, yet it can likewise incorporate different vegetables like carrots or flavors like caraway seeds.

Maturation Time: Sauerkraut regularly matures for a very long time, during which it fosters a harsh and tart flavor.

Taste: Sauerkraut has a milder, less fiery flavor contrasted with kimchi and is much of the time utilized as a topping or side dish.

Kimchi:

Beginning: Kimchi is a conventional Korean dish and is a necessary piece of Korean cooking.

Fixings: Napa cabbage is the most well-known base for kimchi, yet there are different provincial and occasional varieties. Kimchi is known for its incorporation of fixings like garlic, ginger, red pepper pieces, and fish sauce, which give it its particular flavor.

Maturation Time: Kimchi can be prepared in a more limited time contrasted with sauerkraut, commonly aging for a couple of days to seven days. The length can change contingent upon factors like temperature and wanted flavor.

Taste: Kimchi has a complicated and fiery flavor with an equilibrium of pleasantness, harshness, and umami. It is much of the time filled in as a side dish and can be utilized in different Korean dishes.

Both sauerkraut and kimchi are wealthy in probiotics, which are helpful for stomach wellbeing. They are likewise flexible and can be utilized in various recipes, like plates of mixed greens, sandwiches, and stews. The aging system protects the cabbage as well as improves its dietary benefits.

Client

Sauerkraut and Kimchi Maturation recipes

here are fundamental recipes for aging sauerkraut and kimchi:

Sauerkraut Recipe:

Fixings:

1 medium-sized head of white cabbage

1-2 tablespoons of non-iodized salt (genuine or ocean salt)

Discretionary: caraway seeds, juniper berries, or different flavors for some character

Guidelines:

Eliminate the external leaves of the cabbage and put them away.

Wash the cabbage and shred it finely. You can utilize a blade or a cabbage shredder.

In a huge blending bowl, add the destroyed cabbage and salt.

Knead the cabbage and salt together for around 5-10 minutes. This helps discharge the cabbage's juices.

Discretionary: Add flavors like caraway seeds for some character.

Pack the cabbage and squeeze it firmly into a spotless glass container or maturation vessel. Push down to take out air bubbles.

Place one of the held cabbage passes on top to go about as a boundary.

Cover the compartment with a top or a material with an elastic band to keep out impurities.

Permit it to mature at room temperature (around 65-75°F or 18-24°C) for 1-3 weeks, contingent upon your taste inclination.

Taste the sauerkraut incidentally and when it arrives at your ideal degree of tartness, move it to the fridge to dial back aging. It tends to be put away for quite some time.

Kimchi Recipe:

Fixings:

1 medium napa cabbage

1/4 cup non-iodized salt (genuine or ocean salt)

2 tablespoons fish sauce or soy sauce (for a vegan variant)

1-2 tablespoons sugar

1-2 tablespoons ground ginger

4-5 cloves of garlic, minced

2-3 tablespoons Korean red pepper pieces (gochugaru)

Discretionary: vegetables like radish or green onions, cut

Directions:

Slice the napa cabbage down the middle longwise and afterward into scaled-down pieces. Place them in a huge bowl.

Break down the salt in 4 cups of water and pour it over the cabbage. Blend well to guarantee in any event, salting.

Allow the cabbage to sit for 1-2 hours, turning it sporadically.

Wash the salted cabbage with cold water a couple of times and afterward channel it completely.

In a different bowl, blend the fish sauce (or soy sauce), sugar, ginger, garlic, and red pepper drops to make glue.

Join the glue with the depleted cabbage and any discretionary vegetables. Blend everything completely.

Pack the combination into a spotless glass container or maturation vessel, squeezing it down immovably to eliminate air bubbles.

Leave some space at the highest point of the compartment, and utilize a cabbage leaf or weight to keep the kimchi lowered in its juices.

Cover with a top or fabric and let it mature at room temperature for a couple of days to seven days, contingent upon your inclination.

When it arrives at your ideal degree of aging, move it to the cooler to store it for a considerable length of time.

Make sure to sanitize your maturation compartments and utensils to guarantee a fruitful maturation process. Also, taste and screen the maturation progress to accomplish your ideal flavor and tartness.

Pickling with Brine and Fermentation Crocks

Pickling with brackish water and maturation vessels is a conventional food protection strategy that includes utilizing a saltwater answer for aged vegetables or different food sources. Here is a short clarification of every part:

Saline solution: Brackish water is a combination of water and salt, normally around 2-5% salt by weight. It goes about as an additive and establishes a climate where helpful lactic corrosive microscopic organisms can flourish while repressing the development of harmful microorganisms. The brackish water helps protect the food and gives it a tart flavor.

Aging Vessels: Maturation vessels are specific holders intended for aging food sources. They are normally made of stoneware or ceramic and come in different sizes. These vessels have a water-seal or isolated space framework that permits gases delivered during maturation to escape while keeping air from entering, which keeps an anaerobic climate for the aging system.

To pickle with salt water and aging containers, you'd for the most part follow these means:

Set up your vegetables or different food sources by cleaning and cutting them into the ideal shapes.

Make a saline solution by dissolving salt in water to the ideal focus.

Place the vegetables in the aging vessel and cover them with the salt water. You can likewise add flavors, spices, and different flavorings.

Guarantee the vegetables are completely lowered in the brackish water to forestall deterioration.

Seal the container with the top, and the water-seal or isolated space framework will permit gasses to escape while keeping air out.

Allow the container to sit at room temperature for a few days to weeks, contingent upon the recipe and your taste inclinations. During this time, lactic corrosive microbes will normally mature the food, changing it into pickles or other aged delights.

This strategy is generally utilized for pickling cucumbers to make dill pickles, yet you can age a wide assortment of vegetables, like sauerkraut, kimchi, and that's only the tip of the iceberg. It's a characteristic and customary method for saving food and making delectable, probiotic-rich sauces.

Unquestionably! Here is a fundamental recipe for pickling vegetables with salt water and maturation containers. This model proposes cucumbers to make customary dill pickles:

Fixings:

New cucumbers

Water

Fit salt (around 2-3 tablespoons for each quart of water)

New dill (dill heads or twigs)

Garlic cloves

Dark peppercorns

Discretionary flavors like mustard seeds, coriander seeds, red pepper chips

Directions:

Clean and set up the cucumbers: Wash the cucumbers completely and trim off the bloom. You can leave them entire or cut them into lances or coins, contingent upon your inclination.

Set up the saline solution: Break up the legitimate salt in the water to make a saltwater arrangement. Use around 2-3 tablespoons of salt for every quart of water. You'll require sufficient salt water to cover the cucumbers in the vessel.

Layer the vessel: In your maturation container, add a layer of new dill, garlic cloves, dark peppercorns, and any discretionary flavors you like.

Pack the cucumbers: Add the pre-arranged cucumbers to the vessel, pressing them firmly to limit air holes. Make certain to leave some space at the top.

Pour in the brackish water: Cautiously pour the saline solution over the cucumbers until they are lowered. Guarantee there's about an inch of headspace between the brackish water and the highest point of the vessel.

Weight down the cucumbers: Spot a maturation weight or a perfect, food-safe item (like a plate) on top of the cucumbers to keep them lowered under the brackish water. This forestalls shape development.

Seal the container: Put the top on your aging vessel, ensuring it's impermeable and secure.

Maturation: Spot the container in a cool, dull spot (around 65-75°F or 18-24°C) and permit it to age. The term of aging can differ, however, for cucumber pickles, it's regularly 1-3 weeks. Check your pickles routinely, and taste them to see when they arrive at your ideal degree of tartness.

Appreciate: When your pickles have arrived at the ideal degree of maturation, eliminate the weight, seal the container, and store your pickles in the cooler. They will keep on creating flavor over the long haul.

Recall that this is only one model, and you can adjust the recipe as you would prefer inclinations and the sorts of vegetables you need to pickle. The key is to keep a perfect and hermetically sealed climate in your maturation vessel while permitting regular maturation to happen.

Safety and Troubleshooting for Fermentation

Guaranteeing well-being and investigating maturation processes is critical. Here are a few hints:

Security:

Legitimate Ventilation: Guarantee great ventilation to forestall the development of risky gasses.

Individual Defensive Gear (PPE): Utilize suitable PPE, for example, sterile garments, gloves, and security goggles.

Synthetic Taking care of Handle synthetic substances with care and follow well-being information sheets (SDS).

Fire Wellbeing: Be ready for expected fires with fire dozers and fire covers.

Crisis Methods: Know crisis methodology and the area of well-being showers and eyewash stations.

Cleanliness: Keep up with great individual cleanliness to forestall tainting.

Investigating:

Pollution: Distinguish and address any defilement issues immediately.

pH and Temperature: Screen and control pH and temperature as they can influence aging.

Supplement Levels: Guarantee satisfactory supplement levels for the microorganisms.

Air circulation: Appropriately circulate air through the maturation vessel to give oxygen to the microorganisms.

Tumult: Guarantee adequate unsettling for blending and circulation of supplements.

Examining: Routinely test and dissect the aging to check for deviations.

Increasing: Be wary while increasing, as bigger volumes might have various prerequisites.

Here are more security and investigating tips for maturation:

Security:

7. Marking and Stockpiling: Appropriately name and store synthetic compounds and reagents to forestall mistakes.

Garbage Removal: Discard squandered materials, including society media, as per guidelines.

Electrical Security: Guarantee electrical gear is all around kept up with and utilized securely in wet conditions.

Preparing: Train staff in safe aging practices and crisis strategies.

Investigating:

8. Froth Control: Carry out froth control procedures to forestall spills over and misfortunes.

Checking Instruments: Routinely align and keep up with observing instruments for precision.

Stress Variation: Comprehend how microorganisms might respond to as needs be pressure and change conditions.

Testing Procedures: Utilize appropriate aseptic inspecting methods to keep away from tainting during examination.

Information Logging: Keep up with itemized records and information logs for following maturation progress.

Alternate courses of action: Foster alternate courses of action for unforeseen issues like gear disappointments.

Strain Determination: Pick the most reasonable microbial strains for your maturation cycle.

Cleansing Approval: Guarantee legitimate disinfection of hardware and media to stay away from pollution.

Logical Testing: Routinely perform scientific tests to screen item quality and yield.

Recollect that maturation cycles can be profoundly intended for the microorganisms and items included, so adjust these tips to your specific circumstance and counsel specialists when required.

Chapter: 8 Root Cellaring and Storage

Root Cellar Design and Maintenance

A root basement is a kind of underground stockpiling region used to safeguard organic products, vegetables, and other transitory food things. Legitimate root basement plan and support are essential to establish a climate that keeps food cool, sticky, and all-around ventilated. Here are a few key contemplations:

Area: Pick a site that is very much depleted and not inclined to flooding. The basement ought to be arranged underground to profit from the world's regular protection, which keeps a steady temperature.

Protection: Legitimate protection is vital for controlling temperature and mugginess. Use materials like earth, straw, or froth protection to make a very protected space.

Ventilation: Satisfactory ventilation is important to guarantee a constant stock of natural air. Ventilation lines or vents ought to be introduced to take into consideration air trade.

Mugginess control: Root basements ought to keep a high moisture level to keep food from drying out. This can be accomplished by utilizing soaked sand, straw, or different materials on the basement floor.

Racking and stockpiling: Sort out your root basement with racking and stockpiling compartments to keep food things off the ground and forestall deterioration.

Temperature control: The ideal temperature for a root basement is normally around 32-40°F (0-4°C). Contingent upon your area and the season, you might have to change protection and ventilation to keep up with this temperature.

Observing: Routinely check the temperature and stickiness levels in the basement to guarantee they stay inside the ideal reach.

Support of a root basement includes customary reviews, cleaning, and resolving any issues with temperature or mugginess. With legitimate plan and upkeep, a root basement can assist with broadening the timeframe of realistic usability of your local or privately obtained produce.

Surely, here are a few extra subtleties on the root basement plan and support:

Lighting: Root basements are ordinarily kept dull to forestall the development of light-delicate vegetables like potatoes and onions. Utilize low-light or no-light sources, for example, Drove bulbs covered with red or blue film to give negligible enlightenment.

Bug control: Seal any breaks or holes in the basement walls and floor to forestall bothers like rodents from entering. Routinely investigate for indications of irritations and go to proper lengths assuming a perversion happens.

Racking and association: Utilize strong, customizable racking to store various kinds of produce. Keep foods grown from the ground discrete, as some transmit gasses that can influence others. Gather comparative things to make the association and pivot more straightforward.

Root basement types: There are different sorts of root basements, including unearthed basements, barrel root basements, and, surprisingly, changed storm cellars. The sort you pick will rely upon your area, accessible space, and spending plan.

Check produce consistently: Routinely review put-away produce for indications of waste or rot. Eliminate any harmed things to keep them from influencing others. Pivoting your stock guarantees that the most seasoned things are utilized first.

Plan for occasional changes: Be ready to change ventilation and protection as per occasional temperature changes. In colder climates, you could have to add more protection to keep a steady temperature.

Store the right things: Not all leafy foods are appropriate for root basements. Some, similar to apples, carrots, potatoes, and squash, are great competitors, while others might require different capacity conditions.

Record-keeping: Keep a log of what you have put away in your root basement and when it was put there. This assists you with monitoring stock and knowing when things should be utilized or saved.

Recall that a fruitful root basement plan and support might require some trial and error and change because of your particular environment and produce. Appropriately planned and kept up with root basements can broaden the capacity life of your local or privately obtained food varieties, assisting you with getting a charge out of new produce all year.

Absolutely! The following are two or three recipes that are great for fixings normally put away in a root basement:

Root Vegetable Dish:

Fixings:

4-5 cups of root vegetables (carrots, potatoes, parsnips, turnips, and so on), stripped and cut into lumps

2-3 tablespoons of olive oil

2-3 cloves of garlic, minced

New or dried spices (rosemary, thyme, or sage)

Salt and pepper to taste

Guidelines:

Preheat your broiler to 400°F (200°C).

In an enormous bowl, throw the root vegetables with olive oil, minced garlic, spices, salt, and pepper.

Spread the carefully prepared vegetables uniformly on a baking sheet.

Cook in the preheated broiler for 30-40 minutes or until the vegetables are delicate and brilliant brown.

Act as a heavenly side dish.

Potato Leek Soup:

Fixings:

4-5 potatoes, stripped and diced

2 leeks, white and light green parts, cut

1 onion, slashed

2 cloves of garlic, minced

4 cups of vegetable or chicken stock

2 tablespoons of margarine

Salt and pepper to taste

1/2 cup of cream or milk (discretionary)

Guidelines:

In an enormous pot, soften the spread over medium intensity.

Add the slashed onions, leeks, and garlic. Sauté until they become delicate and clear.

Add the diced potatoes and keep on cooking for a couple of moments.

Pour in the stock and season with salt and pepper. Heat to the point of boiling.

Decrease the intensity and let the soup stew until the potatoes are delicate.

Utilize a drenching blender to puree the soup until smooth. If you favor a creamier surface, add the cream or milk.

Change the flavoring on a case-by-case basis and serve hot.

These recipes take full advantage of root vegetables and can be arranged utilizing fixings put away in a very much-kept root basement. Partake in the new kinds of your local produce!

Storing Vegetables without Preservation

Putting away vegetables without conservation commonly includes keeping them in a cool, dry, and very much-ventilated place. Here are a few general tips:

Store at the right temperature: Most vegetables last longer when put away between 32-40°F (0-4°C).

Utilize a root basement: If accessible, a root basement gives an optimal climate to vegetable capacity because of its cool, dim, and high-dampness conditions.

Keep them dry: Dampness can make vegetables decay, so guarantee they are dry before putting them away.

Store independently: A few vegetables produce ethylene gas, which can influence others. Keep ethylene makers like apples from ethylene-touchy veggies.

Utilize breathable holders: Paper sacks, network packs, or punctured plastic sacks can assist with keeping up with air dissemination and forestall dampness development.

Consistently check for decay: Examine your vegetables and eliminate any ruined ones to keep them from influencing others.

Recall that various vegetables have differing capacity prerequisites, so it's crucial to know the particulars for each kind you're putting away.

Surely, here are more ways to store vegetables without protection:

Potatoes, onions, and garlic ought to be put away in a cool, dull spot, but not in the fridge.

Carrots and celery can be put away in the fridge, enclosed by moist paper towels, or set in a holder with water.

Mixed greens like lettuce and spinach ought to be put away in a plastic pack with some air openings to keep up with newness.

Tomatoes ought to be put away at room temperature until completely ready, then, at that point, set in the cooler to broaden their timeframe of realistic usability.

Peppers and eggplants can be put away in the crisper cabinet of the cooler.

Keep winter squashes (e.g., butternut, oak seed) in a cool, dry spot and use them for a couple of months.

Cucumbers and zucchini are best put away in the cooler.

Green beans, snap peas, and asparagus can be kept in the cooler, ideally in a plastic pack.

Mushrooms ought to be put away in a paper sack in the cooler.

Beets, turnips, and radishes can be put away in the cooler with their tops eliminated.

Spices like cilantro and parsley can be put away in a glass of water in the fridge.

Corn ought to be kept in the husk and consumed quickly for the best taste.

Brussels fledglings and cabbage can be put away in the crisper cabinet of the fridge.

Broccoli and cauliflower can be put away in the cooler in a plastic pack.

Yams incline toward a hotter stockpiling region, around 55-60°F (13-16°C).

Store leeks and scallions in the cooler, enveloped by a sodden fabric or paper towel.

Recall that the key is to fit your capacity techniques to the particular requirements of each sort of vegetable to augment their newness and timeframe of realistic usability.

here is a basic recipe that permits you to store vegetables without conservation while making a scrumptious simmered vegetable dish:

Broiled Occasional Vegetables

Fixings:

Various occasional vegetables (e.g., carrots, potatoes, ringer peppers, zucchini, onions, and so on.)

Olive oil

Salt and pepper

Spices or flavors of your decision (rosemary, thyme, paprika, and so on.)

Directions:

Preheat your stove to 425°F (220°C).

Wash and set up your occasional vegetables. You can strip them whenever you want, yet leaving the skins on can add additional flavor and sustenance.

Cut the vegetables into comparative measured pieces to guarantee in any event, cooking. For the most part, 1-inch (2.5 cm) blocks function admirably.

Place the pre-arranged vegetables in a huge blending bowl and sprinkle in with olive oil. Throw the vegetables to cover them equally with the oil.

Season the vegetables with salt, pepper, and your selection of spices or flavors. Be inventive with your flavors to add flavor.

Spread the carefully prepared vegetables in a solitary layer on a baking sheet. Use material paper or a softly lubed skillet to forestall staying.

Cook the vegetables in the preheat broiler for around 25-30 minutes or until they are delicate and have a brilliant earthy-colored tone. Mix them on more than one occasion while simmering for cooking.

Eliminate them from the broiler and let them cool before putting them away.

When the cooked vegetables have cooled, place them in an impenetrable compartment or resealable pack. Store in the cooler for up to 3-5 days.

Partake in your broiled occasional vegetables as a side dish, in plates of mixed greens, or as a fixing for grains like rice or quinoa.

This recipe not only permits you to store your occasional vegetables without safeguarding them, but it additionally upgrades their flavor and prepares them for use in different dishes.

Building DIY Root Cellars

Taking care of vegetables without preservation ordinarily requires saving them for a cool, dry, and specially ventilated place. The following are a couple of general tips:

Store at the right temperature: Most vegetables last longer when taken care of between 32-40°F (0-4°C).

Use a root storm cellar: If available, a root cellar gives an ideal environment for vegetable limit given its cool, faint, and high-suddenness conditions.

Keep them dry: Moistness can make vegetables rot, so ensure they are dry preceding taking care of them.

Store freely: A couple of vegetables produce ethylene gas, which can impact others. Keep ethylene producers like apples from ethylene-delicate veggies.

Use breathable holders: Paper sacks, network packs, or penetrated plastic sacks can help with staying aware of air dispersal and thwart soddenness advancement.

Reliably check for rot: Analyze your vegetables and dispose of any destroyed ones to hold them back from affecting others.

Review that different vegetables have varying limit requirements, so it's pivotal to know the specifics for every benevolent you're taking care of.

Unquestionably, here are more ways of putting away vegetables without assurance:

Potatoes, onions, and garlic should be taken care of in a cool, dull spot, but not in the refrigerator.

Carrots and celery can be taken care of in the cooler, encased by damp paper towels, or set in a holder with water.

Leafy greens like lettuce and spinach should be taken care of in a plastic load with some air openings to stay aware of freshness.

Tomatoes should be taken care of at room temperature until prepared, then, set in the cooler to widen their period of practical ease of use.

Peppers and eggplants can be taken care of in the crisper bureau of the cooler.

Keep winter squashes (e.g., butternut, oak seed) in a cool, dry spot and use inside several months.

Cucumbers and zucchini are best-taken care of in the cooler.

Green beans, snap peas, and asparagus can be kept in the cooler, in a perfect world in a plastic pack.

Mushrooms should be taken care of in a paper sack in the cooler.

Beets, turnips, and radishes can be taken care of in the cooler with their tops wiped out.

Flavors like cilantro and parsley can be taken care of in a glass of water in the ice chest.

Corn should be kept in the husk and consumed rapidly for the best taste.

Brussels youngsters and cabbage can be taken care of in the crisper bureau of the refrigerator.

Broccoli and cauliflower can be taken care of in the cooler in a plastic pack.

Sweet potatoes slant toward a more sizzling storage district, around 55-60°F (13-16°C).

Store leeks and scallions in the cooler, encompassed by a soaked texture or paper towel.

Review that the key is to accommodate your ability procedures to the specific prerequisites of each kind of vegetable to expand their originality and period of sensible ease of use.

here is a fundamental recipe that allows you to store vegetables without preservation while making a delicious stewed vegetable dish:

Seared Infrequent Vegetables

Trimmings:

Different periodic vegetables (e.g., carrots, potatoes, ringer peppers, zucchini, onions, etc.)

Olive oil

Salt and pepper

Flavors or kinds of your choice (rosemary, thyme, paprika, etc.)

Bearings:

Preheat your oven to 425°F (220°C).

Wash and set up your incidental vegetables. You can strip them at whatever point is needed, yet leaving the skins on can add extra flavor and food.

Cut the vegetables into relatively estimated parts of assurance regardless of cooking. Generally, 1-inch (2.5 cm) blocks capability honorably.

Place the set-up vegetables in an enormous mixing bowl and sprinkle it with olive oil. Toss the vegetables to cover them similarly with the oil.

Season the vegetables with salt, pepper, and your determination of flavors or flavors. Be imaginative with your flavors to add flavor.

Spread the painstakingly pre-arranged vegetables in a singular layer on a baking sheet. Utilize material paper or a delicately lubed skillet to thwart remaining.

Cook the vegetables in the preheated oven for around 25-30 minutes or until they are fragile and have a splendid gritty shaded tone. Blend them time and again during stewing for cooking.

Kill them from the grill and let them cool before taking care of them.

At the point when the cooked vegetables have cooled, place them in an impervious compartment or resealable pack. Store in the cooler for up to 3-5 days.

Participate in your seared periodic vegetables as a side dish, in plates of leafy greens, or as a fixing for grains like rice or quinoa.

This recipe not only allows you to store your periodic vegetables without shielding, but it also redesigns their flavor and sets them up for use in various dishes.

The Art of Overwintering Vegetables

Overwintering vegetables includes strategies to safeguard and broaden the reap of specific harvests through the cold weather months. This can incorporate utilizing line covers, cold casings, mulch, and choosing cold-tough assortments.

here are a few central issues to consider while overwintering vegetables:

Cold-strong Vegetables: Pick vegetables that are normally cold-open minded, for example, kale, Brussels sprouts, carrots, parsnips, and leeks. These are bound to endure winter conditions.

Timing: Planting ought to be planned with the goal that vegetables are adult yet not excessively so when winter shows up. Pre-fall or late-summer planting is normal.

Mulching: Applying a layer of mulch around the foundation of your plants can assist with protecting the dirt and shielding the roots from frosty temperatures.

Line Covers: These can protect your plants from brutal climates and hold some intensity. Make certain to utilize breathable covers, so dampness doesn't develop and cause infections.

Cold Casings: These smaller-than-normal nurseries give an optimal climate to overwintering, particularly for additional delicate vegetables.

Snow Cover: Snow can go about as a characteristic protector, shielding your plants from very low temperatures. Notwithstanding, it's vital for screen dampness levels to forestall decay.

Watering: Watch out for dampness levels. Plants might in any case require periodic watering throughout the colder time of year, particularly during droughts.

Bug Control: Be careful about bothers like aphids, which can blossom with overwintering vegetables. Utilize proper techniques to control them.

Recall that the progress of overwintering vegetables relies upon your particular environment and the consideration you give. It's a compensating method for getting a charge out of new produce even in the colder months.

Unquestionably! Here is a basic recipe for an exemplary dish utilizing overwintered vegetables:

Cooked Winter Vegetables

Fixings:

2 cups of overwintered root vegetables (e.g., carrots, parsnips, and turnips), stripped and cut into pieces

2 cups of overwintered brassicas (e.g., Brussels fledglings or kale leaves)

2 tablespoons olive oil

2-3 cloves of garlic, minced

1 teaspoon dried thyme or rosemary

Salt and pepper to taste

Directions:

Preheat your stove to 425°F (220°C).

In a huge blending bowl, consolidate the stripped and slashed root vegetables and brassicas.

Shower the olive oil over the vegetables, and add the minced garlic, dried thyme (or rosemary), salt, and pepper. Throw to cover the vegetables equitably with the flavors and oil.

Spread the vegetables in a solitary layer on a baking sheet. You can utilize material paper for a more straightforward cleanup.

Broil the vegetables on the preheated stove for around 25-30 minutes or until they are delicate and somewhat caramelized, blending them a few times during cooking.

When the vegetables are well broiled, eliminate them from the broiler and serve hot.

This dish features the normal kinds of overwintered vegetables, and the broiling system upgrades their pleasantness and surface. Go ahead and modify it with your #1 spices and flavors. Partake in your local, overwintered vegetable variety!

Chapter 9: Recipes for Canned Vegetable Delights

Canned Tomatoes

Canned tomatoes are a helpful and flexible fix frequently utilized in cooking, particularly for making sauces, soups, and stews.

Absolutely! Canned tomatoes will be tomatoes that have been handled and fixed in a can. They come in different structures, including entire, diced, squashed, and pureed tomatoes. Here are a few central issues about canned tomatoes:

Accommodation: Canned tomatoes are accessible all year, making it simple to integrate the kind of new tomatoes into your recipes, in any event, when they are unavailable.

Flexibility: They are utilized in a great many dishes, for example, pasta sauces, bean stew, soups, and curries.

Long Period of usability: Canned tomatoes have a long period of usability, so they can be put away for a drawn-out period without ruining.

Dietary benefit: They hold the vast majority of the healthy benefits of new tomatoes, including nutrients, minerals, and cancer prevention agents.

Cooking Tips: While utilizing canned tomatoes, it's generally expected to deplete and flush them to eliminate overabundance of sodium or safeguard their juice for a sauce. A few recipes call for stewing them to improve flavor.

Types: notwithstanding fundamental canned tomatoes, you can find fire-broiled, natural, and low-sodium assortments to suit your dietary inclinations and flavor inclinations.

Tomato Glue: Tomato glue is one more canned tomato item, which is thicker and more focused than normal canned tomatoes. Adding extravagance and profundity to sauces is frequently utilized.

Is there a particular part of canned tomatoes you might want to investigate further or a specific recipe you're keen on?

Positively! Canned tomatoes can be utilized in a wide assortment of recipes. The following are a couple of famous dishes that component canned tomatoes as a key fixing:

Exemplary Pureed tomatoes:

Heat olive oil, and sauté garlic and onions.

Add canned tomatoes, basil, oregano, salt, and pepper.

Stew to make a tasty pasta sauce.

Stew:

Earthy-colored ground meat or use beans for a vegan rendition.

Add canned tomatoes, stew powder, cumin, and different flavors.

Stew for a good bean stew.

Minestrone Soup:

Consolidate canned tomatoes, stock, vegetables, and pasta or beans.

Season with spices and stew for a consoling soup.

Tomato and Basil Bruschetta:

Blend diced canned tomatoes in with new basil, garlic, olive oil, and balsamic vinegar.

Serve on toasted roll cuts.

Spaghetti Bolognese:

Make a meat sauce by cooking ground meat with onions and garlic.

Add canned tomatoes, tomato glue, and red wine.

Stew for a rich sauce to present with spaghetti.

Shakshuka:

Stew canned tomatoes with ringer peppers, onions, and flavors.

Make wells in the sauce and poach eggs in it.

Lasagna:

Layer canned pureed tomatoes with lasagna noodles, ricotta cheddar, mozzarella, and ground meat or veggies.

Tomato and Mozzarella Caprese Salad:

Join canned tomatoes, new mozzarella, basil, olive oil, and balsamic coating for an invigorating plate of mixed greens.

Gazpacho:

Mix canned tomatoes with cucumbers, ringer peppers, onions, garlic, and flavors to make a cool Spanish soup.

Canned Tomato Salsa:

Blend canned tomatoes, onions, jalapeños, cilantro, and lime juice for a scrumptious salsa. Canned tomatoes are extraordinarily flexible and can be utilized in endless recipes to add profundity and flavor.

Canned Green Beans

Canned green beans are green beans that have been reaped, handled, and protected by canning. They are normally cooked and fixed in jars with water or saline solution to expand their timeframe of realistic usability. Canned green beans are a helpful and promptly accessible choice for adding green vegetables to different dishes or feasts. They can be utilized in recipes like galoshes, soups, and side dishes.

Canning is a technique for food conservation that includes warming food in a fixed holder to kill or repress the development of microorganisms, guaranteeing the food stays protected to eat for a drawn-out period. For canned green beans, the beans are regularly whitened (momentarily bubbled), pressed into jars, and afterward fixed with water or saline solution. The canning system keeps up with the flavor and health benefits of the green beans. It likewise makes them helpful for stockpiling and use, as they can be put away for a drawn-out period without refrigeration until the can is opened. At the point when you're prepared to utilize canned green beans, you can essentially deplete and warm them as wanted in your recipes.

Absolutely! Canned green beans can be utilized in various recipes. The following are a couple of thoughts:

Green Bean Goulash: An exemplary dish made by blending canned green beans with cream of mushroom soup, broiled onions, and flavors. Top it with additional seared onions and heat until browns.

Southern-Style Green Beans: Stew canned green beans with bacon, onion, and a dash of earthy-colored sugar for a sweet and flavorful side dish.

Green Bean Almondine: Sauté canned green beans with fragmented almonds and a touch of lemon spread for a basic and rich side.

Green Bean Salad: Prepare canned green beans with cherry tomatoes, red onion, feta cheddar, and balsamic vinaigrette for a reviving plate of mixed greens.

Green Bean Pan fried food: Utilize canned green beans in a sautéed food with your decision of protein, like chicken or tofu, alongside garlic, ginger, and soy sauce.

Green Bean Soup: Mix canned green beans with stock and flavors for a fast and simple green bean soup.

Green Bean and Potato Hash: Join canned green beans with diced potatoes, onions, and your #1 flavors, then sauté for a good side dish.

Green Bean and Tomato Saute: Sauté canned green beans with new tomatoes, garlic, and basil for a vivid and delightful side.

Make sure to change the cooking times and flavors to suit your taste and dietary inclinations while involving canned green beans in these recipes.

Canned Corn

Canned corn will be corn that has been reaped, handled, and protected in a can. It is normally cooked and afterward fixed in a can with a fluid, frequently water or saline solution, to keep up with its newness and flavor. Canned corn is a helpful and durable choice for remembering corn for different dishes or getting a charge out of it as a side vegetable.

Absolutely! The following are a couple of straightforward canned corn recipes you can attempt:

Creamed Corn: Intensity a container of corn with a few margarine and cream or milk in a pot. Season with salt, pepper, and a touch of sugar for pleasantness. Stew until it thickens, and you have a delectable side dish.

Corn and Dark Bean Salad: Join canned corn, dark beans, diced tomatoes, red onion, and cilantro. Throw with a dressing produced using olive oil, lime juice, and your selection of flavors. It's an invigorating and sound plate of mixed greens.

Corn Chowder: Make a smooth corn chowder by sautéing onions and celery in a pot, adding canned corn, chicken or vegetable stock, and potatoes. Season with spices and flavors, then, at that point, stew until the potatoes are delicate. Mix in some milk or cream for wealth.

Corn and Cheddar Dish: Blend canned corn in with ground cheddar, mayonnaise, and beaten eggs. Season with salt and pepper, then, at that point, heat in the stove until it's brilliant and effervescent.

Corn Salsa: Make a lively salsa by joining canned corn with diced red and green ringer peppers, red onion, cilantro, lime juice, and a hint of bean stew powder. Serve it with tortilla chips or as a fixing for barbecued meats.

Corn Squanders: Blend canned corn in with flour, eggs, milk, and flavors to make a player. Drop spoonfuls of the player into hot oil and sear until brilliant brown. These make delectable tidbits or bites.

These recipes offer different ways of involving canned corn in your cooking, whether you're searching for a speedy side dish, a serving of mixed greens, or a heartier feast.

10.4 Mixed Vegetable Medley

Canning Salsas and Sauces

Canning salsas and sauces is an incredible method for saving your custom-made recipes. Make a point to follow safe canning rehearses, such as utilizing sanitized containers, and legitimate canning hardware, and following tried recipes to forestall waste.

Positively! Here is an essential recipe for canning tomato salsa:

Fixings:

10 cups of diced tomatoes (around 5 lbs)

2 1/2 cups of hacked onions

1 1/4 cups of hacked ringer peppers

2-3 jalapeño peppers, finely hacked (adapt to zest)

3 cloves of garlic, minced

1 cup of vinegar (5% corrosiveness)

1 teaspoon of salt

1/2 teaspoon of dark pepper

1 tablespoon of sugar (discretionary)

Directions:

Clean your canning containers and tops by bubbling them or utilizing a dishwasher.

In a huge pot, join every one of the fixings, and heat the blend to the point of boiling.

Stew for 10 minutes, mixing at times.

Spoon the hot salsa into the disinfected containers, leaving around 1/2-inch headspace.

Wipe the container edges clean, put the covers on, and screw on the groups until they're fingertip-tight.

Process the containers in a bubbling water shower for around 15-20 minutes.

Eliminate the containers from the water shower and let them cool. You ought to hear the covers pop, demonstrating a legitimate seal.

Take a look at the seals, mark the containers, and store them in a cool, dull spot.

Make sure to follow USDA or your country's food handling rules for canning to guarantee safe conservation. You can likewise find different salsa and sauce recipes online to suit your taste inclinations.

Canning Soups and Stews

Canning soups and stews is a strategy for saving these food sources for long-haul stockpiling. It includes cooking a cluster of soup or stew, then, at that point, fixing it in impenetrable compartments, normally glass containers, and utilizing intensity to make a vacuum seal. This cycle forestalls the development of microorganisms and waste, permitting you to store the soups and stews for expanded periods without refrigeration. It's a famous method for having natively constructed, prepared-to-eat feasts close by and can be particularly helpful for occasional produce or crisis readiness.

Canning soups and stews can be an incredible method for protecting the kinds of custom-made dinners. Here is an essential recipe for canning vegetable soup, yet you can adjust it to your inclinations:

Fixings:

6 cups of diced blended vegetables (e.g., carrots, peas, beans, corn, potatoes)

1 cup of diced onions

1 cup of diced tomatoes

1 cup of cut celery

1 cup of cut chime peppers

1 cup of green beans, cut into 1-inch pieces

1 cup of corn portions

1 cup of cooked pasta or rice (discretionary)

2 cloves of garlic, minced

8 cups of vegetable stock or water

1 teaspoon of salt (change per taste)

1/2 teaspoon of dark pepper

1/2 teaspoon of dried thyme (or different spices of your decision)

Guidelines:

Set up your canning hardware: Wash and clean your canning containers and covers as per the maker's directions.

In a huge pot, join every one of the vegetables, garlic, and stock (or water).

Season the combination with salt, pepper, and dried thyme. Change the flavoring as you would prefer.

Heat the blend to the point of boiling and afterward diminish the intensity to a stew. Cook for around 10-15 minutes, or until the vegetables are delicate.

Assuming you're utilizing pasta or rice, add it during the most recent couple of minutes of cooking.

Cautiously spoon the hot soup into your disinfected canning containers, leaving around 1 inch of headspace at the top.

Wipe the container edges clean, put the tops on, and screw on the groups until they're fingertip-tight.

Process the containers in a bubbling water shower for the suggested time (typically around 20-30 minutes, contingent upon your elevation and container size). Guarantee the containers are completely lowered.

In the wake of handling, eliminate the containers and let them cool on a spotless towel or cooling rack. You ought to hear a "pop" as they seal. Make sure that the covers are fixed by squeezing the middle; on the off chance that it doesn't flex, the container is fixed. Any unlocked containers ought to be refrigerated and consumed within a couple of days.

Store the fixed containers in a cool, dim spot. They ought to be protected to gobble for as long as a year or more.

Kindly note that canning requires severe adherence to somewhere-safe rules to forestall tainting and waste. It's essential to follow legitimate canning methods, particularly for low-corrosive food varieties like vegetables, to guarantee food handling.

Chapter 11: Serving and Enjoying Your Preserved Vegetables

Creative Ways to Use Canned Vegetables

There are numerous imaginative ways of utilizing canned vegetables. Here are a few thoughts:

Vegetable Pan fried food: Join canned blended vegetables in with your decision of protein and sautéed food with a delightful sauce for a fast and simple feast.

Vegetable Soup: Add canned vegetables to your number one soup recipe to help the nourishing substance and add surface.

Veggie Pizza Fixings: Utilize canned cut mushrooms, olives, and artichoke hearts as heavenly pizza garnishes.

Veggie Squanders: Make waste by blending canned corn, peas, or beans with flour, eggs, and flavors, then, at that point, sauté them until firm.

Vegetable Smoothies: Mix canned spinach or carrots into your morning smoothie for an additional supplement.

Pasta Primavera: Consolidate canned peas, carrots, and asparagus with pasta and a velvety sauce for a scrumptious pasta primavera.

Veggie Tacos: Make flavorful tacos with canned corn, dark beans, and diced tomatoes as fillings.

Veggie Salsa: Make a salsa with canned diced tomatoes, corn, and dark beans to present with tortilla chips or as a garnish for barbecued chicken or fish.

Veggie Meal: Layer canned green beans, corn, and cut carrots with cheddar and breadcrumbs to make a soothing goulash.

Veggie Quiche: Utilize canned spinach, mushrooms, or asparagus in a quiche for a speedy and tasty early lunch choice.

Make sure to deplete and wash canned vegetables to diminish their sodium content before involving them in your recipes.

Surely! Here are a few recipes that imaginatively utilize canned vegetables:

Veggie Potato Child Goulash:

Fixings: Canned blended vegetables, potato children, ground hamburger (or meat elective), cheddar, cream of mushroom soup.

Guidelines: Layer potato toddlers, canned vegetables, cooked meat, and soup in a baking dish. Top with cheddar and heat until brilliant brown.

Mediterranean Chickpea Salad:

Fixings: Canned chickpeas, canned artichoke hearts, cherry tomatoes, cucumber, red onion, feta cheddar, olive oil, lemon juice, spices.

Directions: Join every one of the fixings in a bowl, shower with olive oil and lemon squeeze, and season with spices for a reviving plate of mixed greens.

Vegetable and Lentil Curry:

Fixings: Canned blended vegetables, canned lentils, curry glue, coconut milk, onion, garlic, and flavors.

Directions: Sauté onions and garlic, add curry glue, coconut milk, and canned vegetables and lentils. Stew until flavors merge.

Messy Joe Stuffed Peppers:

Fixings: Canned messy joe sauce, canned corn, cooked ground hamburger (or meat elective), chime peppers, rice.

Guidelines: Cut the tops off ringer peppers, and stuff them with a combination of cooked meat, rice, corn, and messy joe sauce. Heat until the peppers are delicate.

Veggie and Bean Quesadillas:

Fixings: Canned dark beans, canned corn, ringer peppers, cheddar, tortillas, flavors.

Directions: Fill tortillas with canned beans, corn, cut chime peppers, and cheddar. Cook on a frying pan until firm.

Zesty Tomato and Dark Bean Soup:

Fixings: Canned diced tomatoes, canned dark beans, onions, garlic, vegetable stock, flavors.

Directions: Sauté onions and garlic, add canned tomatoes, dark beans, vegetable stock, and flavors. Stew for a tasty soup.

Veggie Spring Rolls:

Fixings: Canned water chestnuts, canned bamboo shoots, rice paper coverings, new spices, plunging sauce.

Directions: Fill doused rice paper coverings with canned water chestnuts, bamboo shoots, and new spices. Roll and present with plunging sauce.

These recipes ought to rouse you to get imaginative with canned vegetables in your dinners. Go ahead and adjust them to your inclinations and dietary prerequisites.

Pairing with Other Foods

Matching food sources can make awesome flavor mixes. Here are a few exemplary pairings:

Wine and cheddar: Red wine with matured cheddar or white wine with brie.

Chocolate and strawberries: The pleasantness of chocolate supplements the poignancy of strawberries.

Peanut butter and jam: An exemplary sandwich combo with differentiating surfaces and flavors.

Fish and lemon: Lemon lights up different kinds of fish dishes.

Pasta and pureed tomatoes: The acidity of tomatoes upgrades pasta dishes.

Assuming you have explicit food varieties as a top priority, go ahead and request matching ideas!

Positively! The following are a couple of straightforward recipes that pair various food varieties to make delightful mixes:

Caprese Salad:

Fixings: Tomatoes, new mozzarella, basil leaves, extra-virgin olive oil, balsamic vinegar, salt, and pepper.

Directions: Cut tomatoes and mozzarella, orchestrate them with basil leaves, sprinkle olive oil and balsamic vinegar, and season with salt and pepper for an exemplary Italian match.

Barbecued Chicken and Pesto Pasta:

Fixings: Barbecued chicken bosom, cooked pasta, pesto sauce, cherry tomatoes, and Parmesan cheddar.

Directions: Throw cooked pasta with pesto sauce, add cut barbecued chicken, and split cherry tomatoes. Top with ground Parmesan cheddar.

Peanut Butter and Banana Smoothie:

Fixings: Peanut butter, ready bananas, Greek yogurt, milk, honey, and ice.

Directions: Mix peanut butter, bananas, yogurt, milk, honey, and ice for a rich and nutritious smoothie.

Red Wine and Dim Chocolate Fondue:

Fixings: Red wine, dim chocolate, and arranged scoops (strawberries, marshmallows, pretzels, and so on.).

Guidelines: Liquefy dull chocolate with red wine in a fondue pot, then plunge your #1 treats for a sweet and refined matching.

Sushi Rolls with Soy Sauce and Wasabi:

Fixings: Sushi rolls (e.g., California rolls), soy sauce, and wasabi.

Directions: Serve sushi rolls with a side of soy sauce and a limited quantity of wasabi for an exemplary sushi matching.

Hosting Canning Parties

Facilitating canning gatherings is a tomfoolery and social method for saving food through canning. It includes welcoming companions or family to your home all things considered getting ready, cooking, and can different natural products, vegetables, or different food varieties. Members can gain proficiency with the canning system, share recipes, and bring back home containers of the protected treats they made. It's an incredible method for appreciating each other's conversation while likewise developing an inventory of natively constructed, rack-stable food sources.

Unquestionably! The following are a couple of canning recipes that you can consider for facilitating canning gatherings:

Strawberry Jam:

Fixings: Strawberries, sugar, lemon juice.

Directions: Cook strawberries with sugar and lemon juice, then, at that point, put the jam in cleaned containers.

Dill Pickles:

Fixings: Cucumbers, dill, garlic, vinegar, water, salt.

Directions: Load cucumbers with dill and garlic, cover with a saline solution made of vinegar, water, and salt, then, at that point, can the pickles.

Pureed tomatoes:

Fixings: Tomatoes, onions, garlic, basil, salt, and pepper.

Directions: Cook the fixings together, then, at that point, can the sauce in containers.

Peach Salsa:

Fixings: Peaches, ringer peppers, onions, cilantro, vinegar, sugar, flavors.

Directions: Blend and cook the fixings, then, at that point, can the salsa.

Fruit purée:

Fixings: Apples, sugar, cinnamon (discretionary).

Guidelines: Cook and squash the apples, add sugar and cinnamon, then, at that point, can the fruit purée.

Pickle Relish:

Fixings: Cucumbers, onions, ringer peppers, vinegar, sugar, mustard seeds, celery seeds, turmeric.

Guidelines: Cleave and cook the fixings, then, at that point, can the relish.

Make sure to follow safe canning rehearses, utilize sanitized containers, and focus on handling times and procedures to guarantee the security and life span of your canned merchandise. You can alter these recipes as you would prefer and the inclinations of your visitors at your canning party

Homemade Gifts Using Preserved Vegetables

Custom-made gifts utilizing protected vegetables can be insightful and exceptional. Here are a few thoughts:

Pickle Gift Set: Make a bunch of natively constructed pickles, such as cured cucumbers, carrots, or even salted jalapeños. Bundle them in bricklayer containers with custom names.

Salsa Sampler: Make various hand-crafted salsas utilizing safeguarded tomatoes, peppers, and onions. Bundle them in enhancing containers with tortilla chips.

Vegetable Chutney: Make an exquisite chutney utilizing protected vegetables, flavors, and vinegar. Gift it in little containers with serving ideas.

Matured Sauerkraut: Plan custom-made sauerkraut and bundle it in impermeable compartments. Incorporate a recipe for involving it as a sauce or in dishes.

Appetizer Platter: Collect protected vegetables like artichokes, olives, and cooked peppers into a delightful appetizer platter. Enclose it in a bin or on a wooden board.

Tomato Jam: Make a sweet and exquisite tomato jam utilizing protected tomatoes and flavors. Bundle it in adorable containers for spreading on toast or presenting with cheddar.

Dried Vegetable Blend: Dry out saved vegetables like chime peppers, zucchini, and tomatoes to make a custom vegetable mix. Bundle it in embellishing holders for soups or sautés.

Do-It-Yourself Well drink Unit: Join safeguarded pickles, tomato squeeze, and flavors in a gift box, alongside guidelines for making a delectable Well drink mixed drink.

Protected Vegetable Pesto: Make an exceptional pesto utilizing safeguarded vegetables, spices, and nuts. Bundle it in containers with a note on the most proficient method to utilize it with pasta, sandwiches, or as a plunge.

Canned Soup: Make a good vegetable soup utilizing safeguarded fixings. Can it be in containers with directions for warming and appreciating?

Make sure to customize your hand-crafted gifts with innovative bundling, marks, and directions to make them considerably more unique.

Surely! The following are two natively constructed gift recipes utilizing protected vegetables:

Salted Jalapeño Pepper Jam:

Fixings:

1 cup protected jalapeño peppers, slashed

1 red ringer pepper, finely slashed

1 1/2 cups white vinegar

6 cups granulated sugar

1 parcel of fluid gelatin

Guidelines:

In a food processor, beat the protected jalapeño peppers and red ringer pepper until finely hacked.

In an enormous pan, consolidate the peppers, white vinegar, and sugar. Heat the combination to the point of boiling over medium-high intensity, blending continually.

When bubbling, mix in the fluid gelatin and bubble for 2 extra minutes, proceeding to mix.

Eliminate the pot from intensity and skim off any froth from the surface.

Empty the hot pepper jam into cleaned containers and seal them with tops.

Allow the containers to cool to room temperature before putting them away in the fridge. The jam can be utilized as a topping, coating, or plunge.

Tomato and Spice Bruschetta Blend:

Fixings:

2 cups saved sun-dried tomatoes, slashed

1/2 cup saved simmered red ringer peppers, slashed

1/4 cup saved artichoke hearts, slashed

2 cloves garlic, minced

2 tablespoons new basil, cleaved

2 tablespoons new parsley, cleaved

1/4 cup olive oil

Salt and pepper to taste

Directions:

In a blending bowl, consolidate the sun-dried tomatoes, broiled red chime peppers, artichoke hearts, minced garlic, and slashed spices.

Shower olive oil over the blend and season with salt and pepper. Throw to completely consolidate every one of the fixings.

Spoon the bruschetta blend into an enriching glass container.

Incorporate a note with serving ideas, for example, spreading it on toasted bread, involving it as a pasta sauce, or fixing barbecued chicken or fish.

These saved vegetable gift recipes are flavorful as well as ideal for offering to loved ones. Make sure to store the saved gifts in a cool, dim spot or the fridge for an ideal timeframe of realistic usability.

Chapter: 10 Safety and Shelf Life

Storage Guidelines

Canning and safeguarding vegetables is an incredible method for expanding their timeframe of realistic usability. Here are some broad stockpiling rules for canning and protecting vegetables:

Clean and get ready: Begin with new, excellent vegetables. Wash, strip, and trim them as needed.

Clean gear: Guarantee that all canning containers, covers, and utensils are appropriately disinfected to forestall tainting.

Pick the right strategy: There are different techniques for saving vegetables, for example, canning, pickling, freezing, and drying. Select the strategy that suits the vegetable sort and your inclinations.

Follow a tried recipe: Utilize solid and tried canning or protecting recipes to guarantee security and legitimate conservation. These recipes indicate handling times, fixings, and procedures.

Use canning containers: Use canning containers intended for safeguarding with two-section covers that make a vacuum seal when handled accurately.

Abstain from packing: Pass on the prescribed headspace in the container to consider legitimate fixing and development during handling.

Handling and fixing: Follow the suggested handling times and strategies for your picked protection technique. Guarantee that containers are fixed appropriately.

Name and date: Mark the safeguarded containers with the items and the date of protection for simple ID.

Capacity conditions: Store canned and saved vegetables in a cool, dull, and dry spot, away from direct daylight and temperature changes. The ideal temperature is regularly around 50-70°F (10-21°C).

Check for deterioration: Intermittently review your safeguarded vegetables for indications of decay, like strange smells, shape, or cover swelling. If all else fails, dispose of the items.

Consume inside a sensible period: While appropriately saved vegetables can keep going for quite a while, involving them in the span of a year for ideal quality and safety is ideal.

Continuously allude to legitimate canning and safeguarding assets or talk with neighborhood sanitation experts for explicit rules and suggestions, as they can shift contingent upon the kind of vegetable and conservation strategy.

Shelf Life of Preserved Vegetables

The timeframe of realistic usability of safeguarded vegetables can differ contingent upon the conservation strategy and bundling. Here are some normal conservation techniques and their surmised periods of usability:

Canning: Canned vegetables commonly have a timeframe of realistic usability of 1-2 years when put away in a cool, dull spot.

Freezing: Frozen vegetables can last 8 a year in a standard cooler and, surprisingly, longer in a profound cooler.

Drying/Getting dried out: Got dried out vegetables can most recently a half year to 1 year or more whenever put away in water/airproof compartments in a cool, dry spot.

Pickling: Salted vegetables, like cucumbers or peppers, can keep going for up to 1-2 years when put away in a cool, dull spot.

Maturation: Matured vegetables, similar to sauerkraut or kimchi, can keep going for a long time to a couple of years when kept in the fridge or a cool basement.

It's vital to observe legitimate capacity rules, like fixing compartments firmly and putting them away in proper circumstances, to augment the timeframe of realistic usability of protected vegetables. Continuously check for indications of waste, like off-scents or uncommon surfaces, before consuming.

Labeling and Dating

Marking and dating are significant parts of vegetable protection to guarantee food handling and quality. This is the way to make it happen:

Naming: Use marks or markers to recognize the kind of vegetable and the date it was protected. This assists you with effectively recognizing the items in the compartment or bundle.

Dating: Compose the date when you saved the vegetables on the name. This is urgent for following the newness and well-being of your saved vegetables.

Capacity: Store the marked and dated vegetables in a cool, dull spot, like a storage space or basement, to expand their period of usability. A few vegetables might require refrigeration or freezing for long-haul conservation.

Revolution: When you add new bunches of saved vegetables, try to utilize the more established ones first to forestall decay and waste.

Check for newness: Routinely examine your marked and dated vegetables for indications of waste, such as off scents, surprising surfaces, or shape. Dispose of any things that give these indications.

Legitimate naming and dating assist you with monitoring your saved vegetables and keeping up with their quality for longer periods.

When to Discard Canned Goods

You ought to dispose of canned products assuming you notice any of the accompanying signs:

Harmed or Swelling Jars: If a can is noticeably harmed, scratched, or protruding, it very well may be an indication of tainting or waste, and you shouldn't consume its items.

Strange Smell: Assuming the canned food has an obnoxious or uncommon scent when you open it, disposing of it is ideal.

Unseemly: If the food inside the can has changed variety fundamentally, it could be an indication of deterioration.

Lapsed Date: Check the "best by" or "use by" date on the can. Assuming the date has passed, it's more secure to dispose of the item, albeit canned merchandise frequently stay protected to eat past this date whenever put away appropriately.

Rust or Consumption: Assuming that you see rust or indications of erosion on the can, it's ideal to discard it. This can make you think twice about the uprightness of the can and its items.

Odd Surface: In the event that the surface of the food appears to be strange or disgusting, it's an indication of waste.

Continuously decide in favor alert if all else fails, as eating ruined canned merchandise can prompt foodborne ailment.

Chapter 11: Techniques and Recipes

Pressure Canning Low-Acidity Vegetables

Canning and protecting vegetables is an extraordinary method for broadening their timeframe of realistic usability. Here is a fundamental outline of the strategies and a straightforward recipe for canning vegetables:

Canning Procedures:

Water Shower Canning: Reasonable for high-corrosive vegetables like tomatoes, this strategy includes lowering containers in bubbling water.

Pressure Canning: Utilized for low-corrosive vegetables like green beans or carrots, this strategy requires a tension canner to protect the food securely.

Pickling: A saltwater arrangement of vinegar, water, and salt is utilized to safeguard vegetables like cucumbers, peppers, and then some.

Freezing: While not canning, freezing vegetables is a straightforward protection strategy. Whiten veggies in bubbling water before freezing.

Fundamental Vegetable Canning Recipe:

Here is a basic recipe for canning blended vegetables:

Fixings:

4 cups of blended vegetables (e.g., carrots, beans, peas)

4 cups water

2 tsp salt

Canning containers, tops, and groups

Guidelines:

Wash and set up your vegetables. Cut them into uniform sizes.

Disinfect your canning containers, tops, and groups by putting them in bubbling water for a couple of moments.

In an enormous pot, heat the water to the point of boiling and add the salt.

Pack the pre-arranged vegetables into the disinfected containers, leaving around 1 inch of headspace at the top.

Pour the bubbling salted water over the vegetables, keeping up with the 1-inch headspace.

Eliminate air rises by running a non-metallic utensil around within the container.

Wipe the container edges, put the cleaned covers on top, and screw on the groups until they're fingertip-tight.

Process the containers in a water shower canner or pressure canner as per the suggested time and strain for your particular vegetables.

After handling, let the containers cool on a spotless towel or cooling rack.

Take a look at the seals by squeezing the focal point of the covers. If they don't flex, the containers are fixed. If not, refrigerate the container and use it soon.

Appropriately fixed containers can be put away in a cool, dim spot for as long as a year. Continuously observe wellbeing rules for canning, and counsel modern assets for explicit vegetable conservation times and strategies.

Vegetable Sauerkraut

Vegetable sauerkraut is a matured cabbage dish that can incorporate different vegetables like carrots, onions, and here and there flavors. The essential fixing is cabbage, which is finely destroyed and aged with the assistance of lactic corrosive microorganisms. This maturation cycle gives sauerkraut its unmistakable tart flavor and is a customary food in numerous European cooking styles, especially in Germany. It's generally expected to be utilized as a fixing or side dish and is known for its probiotic properties because of the valuable microorganisms shaped during maturation.

Canning for Long-Term Food Storage

Canning is an incredible technique for long-haul food capacity. It includes fixing food in containers at high temperatures to kill microbes and protect it. You can buy natural products, vegetables, and even meats. Appropriate methods and gear are fundamental to guarantee well-being and food quality. Assuming you have explicit inquiries about canning, go ahead and inquire!

Canning recipes for long-haul food capacity changes contingent upon what you need to save. Here is a fundamental recipe for canning tomatoes:

Canned Tomatoes:

Fixings:

New tomatoes

Lemon juice or citrus extract

Salt (discretionary)

Hardware:

Canning containers with tops and groups

Canning pot or tension canner

Canning instruments (container lifter, channel, and so forth.)

Steps:

Wash and disinfect your canning containers and tops.

Set up the tomatoes by washing, whitening them in bubbling water for 30 seconds, then submerging them in ice water and stripping them.

Cut the tomatoes into wanted sizes and eliminate any imperfections.

Add lemon juice or citrus extract to each container to guarantee appropriate sharpness. Add 1 tablespoon of lemon juice per half-quart container or 2 tablespoons for each quart container.

Pack the tomatoes into the containers, leaving around 1/2 inch of headspace.

Whenever wanted, add salt (around 1/2 teaspoon for every 16-ounce container or 1 teaspoon for each quart container).

Eliminate air rises by running a plastic spatula or air pocket remover device around the container.

Wipe the container edges with a spotless, soggy fabric to guarantee a decent seal.

Put disinfected covers and groups on the containers.

Process the containers in a bubbling water shower canner or pressure canner, following suggested times and tensions for your height and container size. For the most part, you'll deal with pints for 35-45 minutes and quarts for 40-50 minutes in a bubbling water shower canner.

In the wake of handling, eliminate the containers and permit them to cool. Check for a legitimate seal by squeezing the focal point of the covers; if they don't flex, the seal is great.

Store the fixed containers in a cool, dim spot.

If it's not too much trouble, note that this is an improved recipe. While canning different food varieties, particularly low-corrosive food sources like vegetables and meats, you'll have to keep explicit canning rules and handling times to guarantee security.

Infused Oils and Vinegar

Injected oils and spoonfuls of vinegar are culinary fixings made by adding flavorings to the separate base fluids. Implanted oils are made by soaking spices, flavors, or different flavorings in oil, while imbued spoonfuls of vinegar include soaking comparative fixings in vinegar. This interaction gives the kinds of additional fixings into the oils or spoonfuls of vinegar, upgrading their taste and fragrance. They are much of the time utilized in cooking, as salad dressings, and as sauces to add profundity and intricacy to dishes. Well-known models incorporate garlic-injected olive oil or raspberry-mixed balsamic vinegar.

Chapter 12: Conclusion and Resources

Recap and Final Thoughts

Caning and saving vegetables are respected techniques for expanding the timeframe of realistic usability of new produce. Here is a recap and a few last considerations on these methods:

Canning:

Canning includes warming vegetables in containers to kill microorganisms and compounds, trailed via fixing the containers to make a vacuum.

It's an extraordinary method for safeguarding a large number of vegetables, including tomatoes, beans, and pickles.

Canned vegetables can be put away for quite a while, frequently as long as a year or more.

Legitimate disinfection and fixing are essential to forestall waste.

Safeguarding:

Saving vegetables can incorporate different strategies like pickling, maturing, and drying out.

Pickling includes utilizing salt water or vinegar to safeguard vegetables, making tart and delightful outcomes.

Maturation includes utilizing gainful microbes to make probiotic-rich food varieties, similar to sauerkraut and kimchi.

Drying out eliminates dampness, which can broaden the timeframe of realistic usability while holding flavor and supplements.

Last contemplations:

Both canning and protecting are amazing ways of lessening food squandering, setting aside cash, and partaking in the flavor of new vegetables all year.

It's essential to follow safe canning works, including utilizing tried recipes and legitimate sanitization methods.

Explore different avenues regarding various flavors and flavorings to make exceptional safeguarded vegetable dishes.

Partake in the comfort of having home-protected vegetables close by for a speedy expansion to dinners.

These strategies can likewise be tomfoolery and compensating side interest, permitting you to enjoy the kinds of each season.

82071175R00118